COUNSELING
THE CHILDLESS
COUNSELING
COUPLE

WILLIAM T. BASSETT

PRENTICE-HALL, INC., ENGLEWOOD CLIFFS, N.J.

COUNSELING THE CHILDLESS COUPLE

WILLIAM T. BASSETT

PRENTICE-HALL, INC., ENGLEWOOD CLIFFS, N.J.

Counseling the Childless Couple
by William T. Bassett

18310-T

Prentice-Hall International, Inc.
(*London, Tokyo, Sydney, Paris*)
Prentice-Hall of Canada, Ltd.
Prentice-Hall de Mexico, S.A.

Printed in the United States of America

TO
EVA
AND OUR
RANDY AND MELANIE

INTRODUCTION

This series of books represents the most comprehensive publishing effort ever made in the field of pastoral care. These books could not have been published twenty-five years ago, or probably even ten, for the material was not then available. In the past, single books have been available covering different phases of the task. Now we are bringing the subjects together in a single series. Here we present a library of pastoral care covering the major topics and problems that most pastors will encounter in their ministry. Fortunately, not all of these problems need be faced every week or even every month. But, when they are, the minister wants help and he wants it immediately.

These books are prepared for the non-specialized minister serving the local church, where he is the most accessible professional person in the community. It is a well-accepted fact that more people turn to clergy when in trouble than to all other professional people. Therefore, the pastor must not fail them.

Russell L. Dicks
General Editor

PREFACE

In my first pastorate in 1950 I encountered anguished couples who lamented their "fate" which, despite the depth of their religious devotion, "sentenced" them to childlessness. At that time, I concurred with their thinking that such was their irrevocable, God-ordained destiny. My counseling ministry to those who lamented their inability to have children was limited to sympathetic listening and well-intended platitudes.

Nevertheless, my concept of the matchless grace and loving kindness of God could not "come to terms" with such pastoral care. Had I been a good Moslem with the ability to say, "It is the will of Allah," then I could have been content with such blind fatalism. However, this attitude would have permanently closed the door to a resolution of the problem on the grounds that such was their "Kismet." Fortunately, I dared to doubt and to inquire in quest of a pastoral care of the barren which more nearly reflects Him who is Love and Truth perfectly personified.

Since 1950 I have diligently searched for right answers to the problems of the sterile couple. I do not have all the answers, but several perplexing questions have been answered. I still "see through a glass darkly" (1 Corinthians 13:12), but I now see enough to walk with the infertile couple in the presence of God in the confident assurance that the direction is right and the outlook is hopeful.

From the voluminous medical data on sterility, the pastor may arrive at some valuable conclusions, but medical data alone is inadequate from a theological, ethical and practical pastoral perspective. To erase the deficit which is not met by either medical data or other published sources of information on sterility, I have drawn upon twelve years of personal pastoral experience, as well as that of approximately one hundred fellow ministers.

9

Books, pamphlets and articles listed in the Bibliography have been invaluable guides to my thinking and writing on the subject. Direct quotations are documented in the footnotes. All scriptural references are made from the text of The Revised Standard Version of the Bible. To Mrs. John Warren Steen, Jr., for the drawings of the male and female reproductive system, and to all who "planted" and "watered" in any way, I acknowledge sincere thanks, and to God be praise for every "increase" of positive results which this writing may bring.

The names, places and other identifying characteristics in the actual case studies have been fictionalized; similarities with persons living or dead are, therefore, coincidental.

Without the sacrificial cooperation of my wife, Eva, and our two children, Randy and Melanie, this writing would not have been possible. I thank God for them and for his manifold blessings to me through them.

WILLIAM T. BASSETT

CONTENTS

COUNSELING
THE CHILDLESS
COUPLE

ONE

The NATURE Of STERILITY

DESCRIPTIVE DEFINITIONS

The terms *sterility* and *infertility* are used interchangeably, and are defined in keeping with the most common usage of these terms—the failure to conceive or the inability to effect pregnancy.

In the strictest sense of the word, however, "sterility" is absolute in degree and permanent in duration, whereas "infertility," a much broader term, embraces all the variables of barrenness. While the technical difference between these definitions is without relevance to an understanding of this writing, it will help to file them in memory for future reference since, in common usage, *infertility* is achieving increasing prominence and the term *sterility* is becoming obsolete.

Infertility and sterility are not to be confused with impotency, which is the inability to have sexual intercourse, or with virility, which refers to sexual vigor. The husband, for example, may be virile yet sterile, impotent yet fertile, potent and fertile, or impotent and sterile.

The sterile or "childless couple" refers to those who, over a prolonged period of time, unsuccessfully seek conception and are thus involuntarily childless. Apart from the volitional element, the fact that a couple has been childless for a number of years does not necessarily infer a problem of sterility. Although most couples desire children of their own flesh and blood, some do not; presupposing the existence of a sterility problem for the childless prior to ascertaining the facts is therefore precluded. The American Society for the Study of Sterility considers infertility to be a problem when no pregnancy has occurred following a year of coitus without contraception. The initial year of marriage is frequently utilized as an adjustment period prior to attempting conception. Seldom, therefore, is the sterility problem encountered in couples who have been married for less than two years.

Sterility is generally classified as "primary" and "secondary." This writing is limited in scope to the problem of primary sterility in which conception has never occurred, to couples who repeatedly attempt, yet fail, to conceive and who are thus faced with the problem of involuntary childlessness. Secondary sterility, such as miscarriage, stillbirth, "one-child sterility," menopause and a complete hysterectomy preceded by one or more pregnancies, alters the problem of the couple both in kind and in degree, and thus affords a basis for further and separate consideration.

Any communication between the minister and the sterile couple concerning childlessness is herein regarded as "counseling." The setting may be anywhere: over a cup of coffee at a local fountain, at a garden gate or within the privacy of the pastor's study. The number of persons involved is also a variable because both individual and group counseling are needful.

"Pastoral care," the total ministry of the pastor to the barren couple, is pictorially viewed as the canvas in its entirety. "Marriage and Family Counseling" is one large and significant portion of the canvas, and within this section is "Counseling the Childless Couple," a specialized area which, for the barren, is as crucial to the total picture as the shape and expression of the eyes in a portrait of man. In an informal setting in the normal course of conversation, the problem of sterility is usually but one of many which is disclosed by the infertile couple; therefore, while focusing upon the intricacies of infertility, the immediate and broader context is significant for maintaining a proper perspective.

THE PHYSIOLOGY OF FERTILITY

The physiological nature of sterility is a problem with which the medical profession has diligently and commendably labored for many years. So great are the medical achievements that realistic hope is currently offered to at least 50 percent of the childless couples who seek and secure medical aid. New facts are being published bimonthly in the medical journal *Fertility and Sterility,* and the outlook for a favorable prognosis is increasingly optimistic.

While recognizing the obvious physiological aspect of infertility, it is extremely important that no one relegates and restricts this problem to the physiological realm exclusively, because "involuntary" childlessness adversely affects every area of married life. The whole of human life is so inseparably interrelated that one aspect affects all, as in the words of the Scripture, "If one member suffers, all suffer together; if one member is honored, all rejoice together" (1 Corinthians 12:26 RSV).[1] By-products of the basic physiological problem in involuntary childlessness thus make sterility a very complex, multi-dimensional problem which includes psychological, social, religious and legal aspects. Thus, infertility is the concern of a team of professions. Each aspect of infertility is approached developmentally as the infertility problem unfolds in counseling.

An adequate understanding of the nature of sterility must begin with an orientation in the fundamentals of fertility. Unlike the rarely encountered 18-year-old girl who feared that she was pregnant because she permitted her date the limited liberty of a good-night kiss, most teen-agers of our day know more than the basic "facts of life." Almost everyone knows that babies are born as a result of coitus. Beyond that, however, very few persons of any age know even the most elemental facts as they pertain to pregnancy and propagation of human life. A safe presupposition would be for the counselor to proceed as though the counselee knew absolutely nothing on the subject of fertility and sterility. Despite the degree of education of those who are not of the medical profession, nothing should be taken for granted. Accordingly, drawings of the male and female reproductive systems are included in this writing.

The fertility process begins with the male. The testicles produce millions of healthy, active spermatozoa which converge into the epididymis, a coiled duct, and there begin their path in the vas deferens (labeled "vas" on the drawing of the male reproductive system), a tube which leads to the distended receptacle termed "ampulla." The ampulla converges with the two ejaculatory ducts into the urinary passage or "urethra." The spermatozoa, sometimes called the "male seed," pick up needful secretions from the prostate and bulbo-urethral glands and proceed through the urethra and, by orgasmic reflex contractions, the "semen," the spermatozoa which are bathed in secretions, are squeezed out or ejaculated into the vagina near the cervix or "mouth" of the uterus.

[1] All scriptural quotations used in this book are from the Revised Standard Version of The Bible, copyright, 1946, 1952 by the Division of Christian Education, National Council of Churches.

At this point the fertility process shifts to, and continues within, the female reproductive system. Over 300,000,000 spermatozoa, the average "sperm count" of the normally fertile male, then begin their race to the ovum or "egg," and the one that first reaches and penetrates the fertilizable "egg" wins the race to conception and determines the sex of the baby to be. In normal fertility, many spermatozoa or "seed" are placed by ejaculation on the "starting line," the cervix, but they get no farther due to their inability to move. Numerous other "seed" enter the tubes at the cervix of the uterus and begin their upward climb toward the Fallopian tube but fall by the wayside. Several other "seed" keep going and approach the "finish line," the ovum, with only microscopic distance separating them. Whenever the spermatozoa arrive at the Fallopian tube and find no ovum, they mill about the "entrance" of the tube and await the action of the ovary and the ushering of the ovum into the Fallopian tube by means of the finger-like projections of the "fimbria."

With the penetration of the ovum by a spermatozoon the egg becomes fertilized and is then called an "embryo." Pregnancy thus begins in the Fallopian tube, rather than in the uterus, the very moment that a spermatozoon fertilizes the ovum. The embryo is then pushed by hair-like projections down the tube and into the uterus and there it becomes embedded in the "endometrium," the lining of the uterus. The endometrium securely encloses the embryo and develops into a nourishing bag of fluid known as the "placenta," and there in the placenta within the uterus the embryo is housed and fed by the mother through the umbilical cord, which is attached to the placenta, until the baby is born nine months thereafter.

Anything and everything by any and all means which halts or blocks this process prevents fertility. Whenever there is an electrical power failure in the home, such "big items" as power, power line and transformer are first checked. Similarly, fertility should be checked for the proper power of sperm and ovum, for the power line of clear passage throughout the entire tubing without short circuits, and for the transformer of the uterus to see that it can safely carry that which is channeled to it.

The causal factors in infertility are multiple and exist wherever sterile couples are found throughout the world. Quantities, ratios and percentages vary, but the qualitative nature of sterility is consistently observed the world around. This fact is attested to by the 100

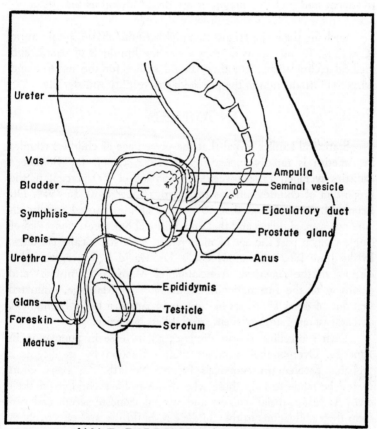

MALE REPRODUCTIVE SYSTEM

doctors from 53 countries who met in New York in 1953 for the "First World Congress on Fertility and Sterility."

A more detailed study of specific causes of sterility are explored in Chapter Four as the couple's medical diagnosis, recommended treatment and probable prognosis are disclosed and as the pastor relates to these couples in their situational needs.

Such are the major factors that highlight the physiological nature of sterility. By no means do they cover the hundreds of details and medical technicalities, but they should suffice for the needful and purposed introduction to the physiology of fertility and sterility.

IN AMERICA

Statistical studies reveal that the percentage of childless couples in America is rapidly increasing. In 1952, Dr. J. Jay Rommer's statistics averaged 15.73 percent, an increase of 600 percent in the proportion of childless unions in America since 1850. In 1954, Dr. Leona M. Bayer found that 16 percent of the married couples in America were childless and that an additional 8 percent, comprised of single women past the age of menopause, were statistically childless. In the June 1962 issue of McCall's, Dr. David R. Mace, executive director of the American Association of Marriage Counselors and chairman of the International Commission on Marriage, estimated that one of every six or seven couples in America today is childless, and at least one-fourth of them are childless by choice.

Each succeeding census discloses an increase in population in America. Overpopulation rather than extinction by sterility is a probable problem in America's future. Nevertheless, every effort should be made to help those who desire to have children of their own. As pastor, social workers and lawyers come to accept and perform their obligations to the childless as faithfully and effectively as physicians and psychiatrists, then hope for the childless will soar to increased heights in a realistic optimism.

Of the childless couples who seek and obtain medical aid, the percentages of pregnancies reported vary from 25 to 65 percent, according to the reports of Dr. L. A. Gray. This is encouraging, but a word of caution is in order. When seeking medical aid, all couples are realistically cautioned that no medical guarantee of pregnancies can be given. Although all *known* causes of infertility may happily re-

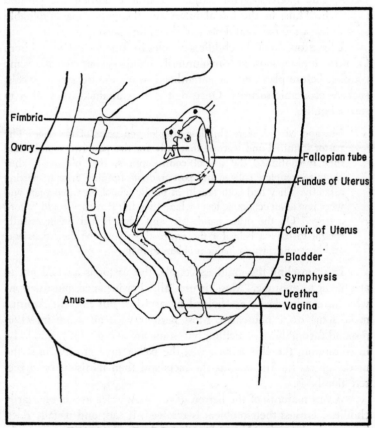

FEMALE REPRODUCTIVE SYSTEM

spond to corrective treatment, there may be unknown or "x" factors which interfere.

Special attention is called to the volitional element in these statistics. Motives and subsequent decisions are basic concerns of the pastor. The motives of the childless couple condition the pastoral approach. Thus, in the initial interview, the pastor may profitably seek to learn the parental desires of the childless couple.

Three-fourths of the childless couples in America desire children. Of this number, most are involuntarily childless; but not all. Some couples, before planning for parenthood, work toward specific goals, such as economic security. Once that goal is attained, they plan to start a family.

> Mr. and Mrs. A were childless after eleven years of marriage. The pastor inquired and learned that only for the past two months had they discontinued the use of contraceptives, that previously they chose to complete college and post-graduate training prior to starting a family. They had both taught in public school for three years and were just at an economic level where they felt that they could "afford a baby." On the other hand, Mr. and Mrs. B had unsuccessfully sought to have a baby for the entire three years of their marriage, and barrenness was a major problem to them.

In counseling the childless couple, the pastor is advised not to assume or to presume. "Most" is not "all." For instance, most persons who have a headache are helped by aspirins, but not all. Aspirins make some quite nauseated. Most persons with an acute infection respond favorably to penicillin; but, some are allergic to it. Similarly, in counseling the childless couple, the pastor may grossly "miss the mark" unless he first obtains the facts and then ministers on a prescription basis.

A vast majority of the barren wives in America are involuntarily childless. Unless their problem is resolved, it can, and usually does, increase in intensity. Very often it reaches a devastating climax in personality distortion at menopause. For instance:

> Mrs. J loved children. All the children of the neighborhood loved her, and she was much in demand by parents and children as a baby sitter. At menopause she turned against children. She no longer wanted any of the "pesky, noisy kids" around her. Several of the children were stunned at first that their "second Mom" had changed so much, but later they gave back in kind to the "crabbed old witch."

An apparently wholesome adjustment to childlessness does not necessarily disclose the feelings of the heart. The pastor is cautioned not to equate inner desires with outward appearances. Pastoral initiative in caring for such couples is thus indicated when the problem is in its incipient stage.

One-fourth of the childless couples in America do not desire children and are using various means to prevent pregnancy. While this may not be a sterility problem, pastoral care is indicated. Those, for example, who see vocation and parenthood as an "either-or" situation may be helped in pastoral counseling to see additional alternatives with "both-and" possibilities. Some who have lost loved ones in warfare are opposed to parenthood lest their children become "cannon fodder" and they be confronted with "unbearable" grief. In pastoral counseling such persons may achieve insights which relieve them of morbid grief. A few "middle-class" couples who experienced dire poverty in early youth state that they do not wish to chance bringing children into similar situations. Pastoral counseling may sometime show such thinking to be rationalizations which are masks for deeper motivations. Yet others may flippantly assert that they do not want children because they are "too much trouble" or they "tie you down to too dull a life." This may be a "front"; hence the pastor is not to misinterpret and disregard them by blindly accepting such statements at "face value." Even when these people are taken at "face value," they can benefit from pastoral guidance.

An interview by the pastor of all couples under his care who are childless after two or more years of marriage is suggested. The pastor will thereby learn how they feel about becoming parents. Those couples under greatest pressure because of infertility will then merit his priority. As the situation indicates, all should be interviewed for an insightful and supportive or corrective ministry.

REGIONALLY

In addition to the physiological aspects of infertility which apply throughout America, environmental factors within a given region may either hinder or help fertility.

Experiments reveal that extremely hot regions have a direct and adverse action on the male testis and an indirect action on the thyroid; that direct exposure to extremely cold, sub-zero temperatures can so immobilize the male "seed" that the husband becomes as barren as a frostbitten fruit tree, and that the optimum temperature for fertility is 65° F. Hence, regions of extreme temperatures are lower in fertility than those of moderate climates.

Couples contemplating a change of residence to a climate more conducive to conception should also consider altitude. Even fertile transients who move to a mountainous region sometime become and remain infertile until they are adjusted to the altitude. Fortunately, however, such infertility is temporary. No impairment to fertility is noted among the acclimated natives of mountainous regions. Some medical authorities also hold that high humidity is harmful to fertility. Moving to humid, low-altitude regions is not recommended for couples who are in quest of a more favorable fertility prognosis. To prevent temporary infertility, couples should avoid relocating in regions where the altitude is drastically different from that of their present one.

Densely populated urban and industrial regions have the highest sterility ratio; sparsely settled rural and agricultural regions, the lowest. Why this is true is noted in the local areas and communities which comprise these regions.

LOCALLY

The principal means of livelihood in many states and counties is agriculture. In these rural areas most of the food that is placed on the table consists of vegetables from their gardens, eggs from their chickens, milk from their cows, beef from their butchered calves and pork from their hams in the "smokehouse." The rural family's appetite is whetted by energetic "out-of-doors" work to the extent that any and all foods which are placed before them are devoured with zest. Sterility resulting from malnutrition or vitamin deficiency is, therefore, seldom encountered among farmers.

Simplicity of life, temperance in all things and the avoidance of excesses pays rich dividends in terms of good general health and a high fertility rate. Deviations toward harsh primitiveness on the one hand or cultural complexity on the other hampers fertility in direct proportion to the degree of the deviation.

In almost every locale in America today, the social and cultural trend is toward higher living standards, better homes and furnishings and smaller families. More and more couples are delaying marriage and a family until they can complete their education and achieve a higher economic standing. Many pass their fertility peak or "prime of life" before their first child is born. Having waited too long, they become either sterile or contentedly set in their ways without children.

Some religious faiths favor large families and oppose the use of contraceptives. Their influence is felt, but no marked difference is noted thereby on the statistics of childlessness. States in which such faiths are predominant have only a slightly lower percentage of infertility than those without this religious factor. Whatever the religious faith, the same physiological principles apply. For instance, densely populated states comprised of large industrial cities have a much higher percentage of infertile couples than those of sparsely settled agricultural states.

COMMUNITY

Despite a surplus of many foods in America, there are the poor in almost every community who are financially unable to afford a balanced diet. In the same community, one finds those who have the means but not the desire to eat a high-protein diet with a minimum of fat-forming materials. One may lose weight while the other gains, but both are on a semi-starvation diet, and a serious deficiency in vitamins A, D and E causes a marked loss in semen quality and can result in male sterility.

As a general rule, the larger the city the smaller the birthrate. Several factors account for this decrease in fertility. Sedentary workers, for instance, do not get enough exercise to adequately stimulate the reproductive system. The larger the city, the larger or more numerous the "red light" districts of prostitution, and, despite antibiotics, doctors' advice to "be careful" and ministers' exhortation to "be good," sterilization by latent gonorrhea continues. While fewer persons are currently sterilized by venereal diseases than in the years preceding penicillin, the ratio is proportionate to exposure. Pressures of the pace of life are also frequently "stepped-up" in the larger cities by long hours, overwork, nervous exhaustion and overindulgence in alcohol, tobacco, carbonated beverages, caffein and sexual stimuli. An increasing number of wives work sixteen hours a day: eight hours outside and eight hours inside the home. In addition to decreased fertility from impaired general health and from excessive acidity caused by stress, they neither find the time nor the energy for coitus. In brief, to promote fertility, avoid excesses and be temperate in all things.

Some industrial communities have a multitude of sterile couples due to occupational hazards. Working with phosphorus, lead, platinum, borox and even sodium chloride may sometimes result in sterility. Electric welding may lead to sterility, and natural gas can seriously damage the female ovaries. Radar is not dangerous because there is no contact with the rays, but direct contact and overexposure to atomic radiation definitely sterilizes. Sometimes x-rays are valuable in treating female infertility, but x-rays on the male testis in sufficient quantities sterilize.

In a few communities heredity is a factor in low fertility. Due to isolation, race, culture, creed or ignorance, some families select their mates from blood relatives. The rate of sterility is known to increase with each succeeding generation of inbreeding.

CHURCH

Probably in every established church there are some who are burdened by barrenness. Many pastors and their wives may be numbered with the involuntarily childless inasmuch as infertility is more frequently found among those in professional vocations. In a representative church membership, an average of one of every eight couples in the churches throughout America are involuntarily childless.

Many infertile couples of the church are above average in intelligence and in faithfulness to church functions. Several own their own homes and frequently they are financially frugal. Most of them consult neither their pastor nor their physician concerning their sterility, and rarely is their barrenness mentioned publicly by anyone of the church.

In some churches the "hands off" hush on discussing sterility is one of deathly silence. The taboo on discussing sexual relationships never achieved as strong a hold in the churches as that of the fruitlessness of these unions. In the recent past even the fruitfulness of conception within marriage was silenced, and the pregnant wife remained in semi-seclusion or "hiding."

Several childless pastors have consulted with the writer seeking information and guidance for themselves, as well as for their parishioners. All were gratified that something positive could be done. A few pastors, however, who had children of their own, expressed to the writer their disapproval of doing anything other than making referral to the family physician. "Clues" to the pastor's attitudes are conveyed on every contact with others by what he says and the way he says it, and by what he does not say. No pastor who "brushes off" deep problems such as sterility with a shallow suggestion should, therefore, be surprised that he rarely has the opportunity for counseling people with such problems.

Despite all opposition and stumbling blocks, however, the pressures of the problem become so strong that a few seek and obtain help. They, in turn, often encourage other childless couples to seek help.

For over ten years, a steady stream of articles written by leading medical authorities on the subject of sterility has come before the public. These popularly written articles have done much to encourage and enlighten. Consequently, the "dark ages" for the barren is ending as pastors perceive and perform their needful counseling ministry. Childless couples need no longer suffer in silence and bear their burdens alone.

TWO

PASTORAL COUNSELING PRIOR
To MEDICAL DIAGNOSIS

BARRIERS TO COMMUNICATION

Communication is prerequisite to pastoral care, and barriers to communication must be overcome before the pastor can counsel or refer the couple. The pastor's first task in ministering to the sterile couple is to remove the impediments to a free and full expression of their problem. Barren couples will frequently disclose to pastor and friends their volitional choice in parenthood, but further disclosures are usually so frustrated with barriers that the couple are unable to communicate their problem.

In counseling the childless couple, the pastor first needs to know their parental desires, because these desires indicate the type of problem with which he is dealing and, accordingly, condition his approach. Upon completing the survey and learning the parental desires of the childless couples, the pastor next needs to learn the motives and beliefs which support their desires for children. Unless there is full and open communication, however, the basic facts essential to imparting insights will not be fully and accurately known.

In ministering to infertile couples, the pastor should be prepared to encounter strong defensive attitudes which guard against disclosure of sexual intimacies, together with confused thinking about reproduction.

In reply to probing questions in the initial visit of a "new" pastor concerning sexual intercourse in timing the ovulation cycle, Mr. W said to his pastor, "Sure, we want a baby of our own, but I don't want to talk about it. It's just something you don't talk about! It's no use anyway. You're either going to have a baby or not, and that's all there is to it. So, why talk about it?" The pastor, unprepared for this defensive and fatalistic reaction, was bewildered and defeated before he started, and the subject was never reopened by either.

To facilitate communication, the pastor must meet the prerequisite of earned and respected confidence. A directive approach of probing questions is likely to meet with failure until this prerequisite is met. The strength of the interpersonal relationships in counseling conditions the amount of stress which it can withstand. The veteran pastor knows that it is far better to wait and to enhance rapport before plummeting the depths of sensitivity than to endanger a complete and permanent break in the counseling relationship.

Communication may be facilitated by clarifying its purpose. In the instance of Mr. W, the initial and indicated need in pastoral counseling was to uncover misconceptions and then progress toward insightful truths. Instead of retreating from the hostile reactions of Mr. W, the pastor appropriately faces the problem with him. Together they seek clarification of Mr. W's fatalistic attitudes. Such an approach logically leads to a confrontation of basic theological concepts of the nature of God and of His purposes of marriage.

The pastor is recognized as an authority on theological and ethical issues, an expert who imparts theological information and interpretations. Laymen feel the need to discuss their religious needs freely with their pastor who, in turn, is ethically obligated to relate their ideals and goals to the truths of Scripture. As the pastor functions clearly within this realm of his professional competence, he furthers communication and spiritual growth.

The physiology of reproduction together with its sexual intimacies are the spheres of the physician, and the pastor is usually blocked by resistance and faced with failure when he assumes the medical role of diagnostician and therapist. Outside of his spiritual role, the pastor often experiences apprehension, and is, himself, unable to communicate freely and accurately. In his religious role, the pastor, in contrast to the physician, has a natural and unique entrée to the problems of the sterile couple. Having united the couple in matrimony, the pastor is generally expected to show concern about the fertility or infertility of these unions. It is not amiss that he be concerned with their motives for pregnancy, the religious doctrine of vocation as applicable to the couple, their theological concepts of sterility, together with the Scriptures upon which they base their convictions, and their prayers to God concerning their barrenness. Within his religious role, the pastor thus finds a unique and strong resource for facilitating communication.

To save time, to give pertinent information both to husband and wife, to clarify theological and ethical concepts and to explain the implications of alternatives, the pastor should interview the couple together. Such a meeting with the couple will enable the pastor to observe their interpersonal relationship, note the degree of cooperation of both and clarify information received when counseling each separately. Such an approach is especially helpful during the initial and final phases of counseling.

Some things the mates will not disclose, however, in the presence of the other relate to misconceptions about sex, hostilities and confessions of sin. To facilitate full communication of their problem, the pastor should counsel the husband and the wife separately under conditions of complete privacy. The counselee will welcome assurance that what is disclosed will be kept in strict confidence, and that they will not be overheard. The usual defenses against misunderstanding ears and condemning hearts are more readily dropped, and communication is thus enhanced when such assurance of privacy is given.

MISCONCEPTIONS

As the couple begin to relate their problem, the pastor imparts information and interpretations which serve to clarify and to correct their theological and ethical misconceptions. Their most prevalent and probably their most important concepts are the often erroneous beliefs that God wills their childlessness, that their barrenness is not to be questioned or that, except for the normally expected conjugal relationships, both human responsibility and creaturely efforts are excluded. These widespread misconceptions are supported in many church circles with the prejudice which opposes the exercise of responsible reason and determined action toward overcoming sterility as interference with divine providence. The assumption is that true piety and reverence for God leaves conception to chance. Such concepts are harmfully erroneous and should be corrected.

Many assumptions about sterility blaspheme the nature of God, who far exceeds the good in the best of parents. "If you then, who convictions, and their prayers to God concerning their barrenness. Within his religious role, the pastor thus finds a unique and strong resource for facilitating communication.

To save time, to give pertinent information both to husband and wife, to clarify theological and ethical concepts and to explain the implications of alternatives, the pastor should interview the couple together. Such a meeting with the couple will enable the pastor to observe their interpersonal relationship, note the degree of cooperation of both and clarify information received when counseling each separately. Such an approach is especially helpful during the initial and final phases of counseling.

Some things the mates will not disclose, however, in the presence of the other relate to misconceptions about sex, hostilities and confessions of sin. To facilitate full communication of their problem, the pastor should counsel the husband and the wife separately under conditions of complete privacy. The counselee will welcome assurance that what is disclosed will be kept in strict confidence, and that they will not be overheard. The usual defenses against misunderstanding ears and condemning hearts are more readily dropped, and communication is thus enhanced when such assurance of privacy is given.

MISCONCEPTIONS

As the couple begin to relate their problem, the pastor imparts information and interpretations which serve to clarify and to correct their theological and ethical misconceptions. Their most prevalent and probably their most important concepts are the often erroneous beliefs that God wills their childlessness, that their barrenness is not to be questioned or that, except for the normally expected conjugal relationships, both human responsibility and creaturely efforts are excluded. These widespread misconceptions are supported in many church circles with the prejudice which opposes the exercise of responsible reason and determined action toward overcoming sterility as interference with divine providence. The assumption is that true piety and reverence for God leaves conception to chance. Such concepts are harmfully erroneous and should be corrected.

Many assumptions about sterility blaspheme the nature of God, who far exceeds the good in the best of parents. "If you then, who are evil, know how to give good gifts to your children, how much more will your Father who is in heaven give good things to those who ask him?" (Matthew 7:11, RSV). Since God's will operates within the actual rather than the presumed limitations of the childless couple, the pastor rightfully leads the couple to realistic appraisals based upon known and discernible facts. Neither pastor nor counselee should take circumstantial evidence of what "seems to be" in a given instance of infertility and malign the Lord by attributing to Him heinous purposes which are alien and opposite to His nature.

In addition to the nature of God, the nature of man is significant to an understanding of God's will in fertility and sterility. God created man in His own image and God was very pleased with mankind, His supreme creation (Genesis 1:27–31). The adult body which functions as God originally made it has the power to create life in God's own image. The adult mind as created by Him is capable of thought and forethought which lead to valid conclusions. The adult "will" or volition is capable of charting and following a course which uses these God-given powers aright. To strengthen or to regain these natural powers by means of modification and even contrivance, therefore, is working with the Creator. So thinking, the pastor can strengthen childless couples by supporting their efforts to correct infertility as reverent trust in God rather than as a negation of faith in divine providence.

Adequate pastoral care of the sterile couple seeks to discover the roots upon which the couple base their convictions concerning the will of God in childlessness. Their convictions may be superficial or faulty, and may thus require uprooting and replanting on a sound basis.

> Mrs. D, age 31, after seven years of involuntary childlessness, stated to her pastor, "It doesn't seem fair. Look at the J family. He comes home drunk half the time, lets his children go ragged and hungry, never goes to church, lives like the devil, and they have seven children. Or take the C's. He gambles and 'steps out' on his wife, and they have four children. I know I've sinned, but I don't think I've done as much to deserve punishment as they have . . . but they have children and we don't. Why . . . I want to know . . . Why?" The pastor, slowly shaking his head in negation, replied, "I don't know, but I do know that God is just and, as the song goes, 'we'll understand it better bye and bye.'"

its life, but it is extraneous to the "one flesh" (Genesis 1:28; 2:24–25; 9:1). "Be fruitful and multiply" refers to a blessing rather than to a command of God which may prove impossible to obey. The minister officiating in marriage may thus pray that the union be "blessed" with children, but he does not lead them to make marriage vows which contain an exemption clause for sterility. The Scriptures teach that the couple shall be one until death, and sterility is not mentioned as an exception to the permanency of marriage.

The erotic element within marriage is primarily a means of expressing love which is of ethical significance independent from and possibly more meaningful than sex as a means of procreation. Apart from procreative purposes, human sexuality embraces far more than animal instinct which is subhuman. By the use of such passages of Scripture as 1 Corinthians 7:5 and Matthew 19:6, the pastor justly supports the complete expression of conjugal love.

The biological needs of the virile oppose divorce and subsequent celibacy which, in turn, denies the fulfillment of the couple's physical potential for communicating their emotions of love and unity. To endorse divorce on the basis of sterility is to support an erroneous theology which is based upon the dichotomy of body and spirit. Body and spirit are one; therefore, married couples are not sinning by giving bodily expression to their oneness of spirit. Since sterility seldom prevents conjugal fellowship, the "one flesh" in marriage, which is a new creation of unity ordained of God for permanency, is not broken by sterility. Sterility is not, therefore, an ethical basis for divorce, and the pastor should firmly negate divorce as an ethical solution to the sterility problem.

While some infertile couples do not subscribe to divorce, they do maintain that the only justifiable purpose of coitus is procreation. Those who hold such views believe that the only morally justifiable times to have sexual relations are on days when conception is most likely to occur. In addition to their erroneous concept of the purposes of marriage, they are practicing an ethic of expediency, a relative standard without Scriptural authority. By correcting their basic presupposition concerning the purposes of marriage, the ethic of expediency is automatically eliminated. In fulfilling his religious role, however, the pastor should bring light to bear upon both errors.

As the couple work through their theological and ethical misconceptions with their pastor, confidence often increases, and they usually communicate more freely their intimate, physiological problems. Although it is not the pastor's role or task to go into the details of the physiology of reproduction, when sufficiently informed, he can and should negate medical misconceptions which stifle initiative and the subsequent resolution of the infertility problem.

The pastor frequently encounters the misconception that potency verifies fertility and that the wife is thus totally responsible when the union proves childless. The husband, however, may sometimes erroneously fear that the size of his sexual organs influences fertility.

> Mr. C said, "Preacher, my wife has been to see the doctor. He says she's all right. She wants me to go, but I don't think there's anything wrong with me. I haven't had any diseases to foul me up. I'm healthy, and I don't have any trouble being a man to my wife." The pastor called to his attention a man whose "tubes" were "tied off," who was virile yet infertile, and who could say equally as much of his relations to his wife. Then, laughing nervously, Mr. C said that maybe his penis was not long enough to effect pregnancy. Dubious of this conclusion, the pastor replied that the only sure way to determine his fertility or his capacity to impregnate was by consulting a medical authority for fertility tests and detailed information. The pastor supported his referral with the assurance that it would be better to know for sure than to remain in doubt. Mr. C thought it over and decided to make an appointment for fertility testing.

The pastor usually encounters either opposition or reluctant cooperation from the husband until their relationship is fully structured and the needs are clearly understood. Thereafter, cooperation from the husband is normally assured.

To enlist the cooperation of some infertile wives, the pastor must correct the misconception that infertility treatment is usually, if not invariably, surgical and dreadfully complicated in nature.

> Mrs. S referred to a middle-aged friend who was unsuccessfully treated for infertility by surgery, and who now has considerable gynecological complications. Mrs. S stated that she did not want to take such a risk. The pastor assured her that it would be helpful to get expert medical advice and that, currently, surgery was seldom necessary or advised as treatment. He reminded her that the option to accept or to reject surgery, when advised, was left to the decision of the patient.

Rather than to be content with presumptions which may be totally or partially erroneous, in each instance which involves medical concepts, whether false or true, the pastor is urged to refer the couple to the appropriate medical authority.

SELF-DIAGNOSIS

Throughout the initial phase of counseling the childless couple, the pastor generally encounters the self-diagnostic assumption of the couple that, apart from medical findings, they know not only their biological condition but also their therapeutic needs. Many childless couples, for instance, regard themselves as hopelessly sterile after one or two years of unsuccessful attempts to conceive a child, while others believe that they are "normal" and that, eventually, conception will occur without recourse to aid. Self-diagnosis is unfounded faith, wishful thinking, fixity which is borne of prejudice, and fatalistic disregard of conditioning factors. Self-diagnosis, as the above definitions indicate, is basically a psychological problem, and the pastor errs who approaches the problem first, primarily or exclusively on the basis of its ethical implications.

Fear of diagnostic findings may motivate a self-diagnosis of potentialities or of limitations. The male ego, for instance, fears lest the results of diagnosis reveal that he has harmed himself, and regards sterility as a shameful stigma of weakness which places him in a subordinate role and which casts a reflection of failure upon his manhood. An exploration of the emotional roots of the couple's diagnostic presuppositions is a vital need in pastoral counseling.

In a strong relationship of confident trust, and upon the inquiry of his pastor as to what was holding him back from fertility tests, Mr. C said, "Preacher, it's not the money. I'll be frank with you. I'm afraid of what I'll find out." The pastor asked, "Why should you fear the truth?" Mr. C then confessed to marital infidelity, quickly adding that he had never contracted a venereal disease, and expressed apprehension of being "played out." Confessions continued with details of his sexual exploits and "conquests." The pastor then stated his ethical conviction that marital fidelity should precede parenthood, and asked if Mr. C felt convicted of sin and if he had now made a change. Mr. C and his pastor then prayed for God's forgiveness and for Mr. C's return to marital fidelity. Mr. C rose from his knees in happiness, marred only by this apprehension:

"Should I tell my wife how I've been living? I'd rather not if I don't have to, but if my tests show up bad, she may wonder." The pastor had learned that Mrs. C's love for her husband was strong and that she already suspected him of infidelity. Since Mr. C had confessed to God, he and his pastor agreed that it would serve no constructive purpose to confess to her, and they agreed that if she did find out, then to be examined would be better than to "hold out" on her. Mr. C then committed himself to see the doctor for semen analysis.

The husband tends to overconfidence, whereas the wife tends to underconfidence. The wife, for instance, may be inclined to fear permanent sterility as punishment for sin.

Mrs. C was continually depressed and frustrated. Feeling that God was punishing her for sin, she diagnosed herself as hopelessly sterile. This diagnosis was objectively supported only by her involuntary childlessness after two years of unsuccessful efforts. Upon the query of her pastor as to why God should punish her, she confessed to premarital sexual relations with her husband during the engagement period. She concluded that for this sin God was denying her of that which she desired more than anything else, namely, children of her own. She felt "misunderstood" and "all alone." She wanted to have a girl who looked like her, and she wanted to rear her daughter far differently from the way that her mother reared her. The pastor listened in prayerful attentiveness until she had bared her soul completely. He then led in prayer for forgiveness and reconciliation to God. Mrs. C then stated that she wondered if she and her husband were mismated, but this doubt was resolved in response to the pastor's leading her to an examination of her feelings for Mr. C prior to their premarital sexual relations and to a reconsideration of the sincerity with which she took the marriage vows. Rather than to accept personal presumptions, the pastor recommended that Mrs. C consult a physician to see if her fears of permanent sterility were biologically founded. He also confronted her with her inordinate desire for children as possible idolatry.

Confession is vital to the pastoral care of the sterile couple. Reconciliation to God and to each other should precede parenthood, and idolatrous desires for children should be destroyed. At the same time, since God's creative laws are consistent for both the moral and immoral, the pastor may render a significant service by relieving the couple of inordinate and unjustifiable feelings of guilt.

The pastor frequently encounters and, in his teaching ministry, seeks to correct negative motives for pregnancy. The desire for children to satisfy the husband, to stabilize a "shaky" marriage, to be like others, to have "something" of their own to love them and to show their mothers how to rear a child, are five prevalent negative inducements to pregnancy which the pastor encounters in counseling the childless couple.[1] The pastor's task is to lead them from negative and idolatrous motives which exploit and manipulate a child for selfish purposes to motives which value the child for, and of, himself.

As a representative of God, the pastor is obligated to seek the destruction of idolatrous desires for children by confirming with the barren couple the sovereignty of God. Through his teaching ministry, he instructs them in the relative values for time and eternity. He seeks to facilitate the acquisition of new insights which correct their value judgments, so that they come to be centered and unified in the sovereignty of God and the Lordship of Christ, in the "hierarchy of love" which enables them to function constructively. This portion of counseling is successfully completed when the couple come to pray from the heart the following prayer:

> "O Thou who dost smile with approval upon our desire for children, save us all from the idolatry of that desire. Grant these thy servants the sense of peace and serenity that comes from surrender of every defective motive for wanting children."[2]

To relieve feelings of depression and frustration of such persons as Mrs. C, the pastor seeks to promote insights which help them to recognize and to affirm their humanity through an accurate appraisal of their personal limitations, failures and potentialities. The pastor is not to create the illusion of an earthly paradise which is divested of tribulation, tension and responsibility; neither is he to affirm or to imply that finite life is a heavy yoke of iron which is hopelessly permanent. Should, for instance, Mrs. C actually be permanently sterile, the pastor may appropriately reassure her that participation in the perpetuation of the human race may be achieved within the vocational will of God for her life by means other than pregnancy, and thus allay her apprehension of finitude. To remove her moun-

---

[1] See E. S. Ford and I. Forman, "A Psychodynamic Approach to the Study of Infertility," *Fertility and Sterility*, 4 (6):459, November–December, 1953.
[2] Wayne E. Oates, *Where to Go for Help* (Philadelphia: The Westminster Press, 1957), p. 70.

tainous obstacles of disappointment, loneliness and tragedy, the pastor endeavors to lead her from fatalistic, stoic resignation, to faith borne of transcending love for God.

Blessed is he who is characterized by the courage to risk confrontation and self-affirmation in the presence of God whose Spirit of "perfect love casts out fear" (1 John 4:18). This is the ideal atmosphere, temperature and humidity in counseling the childless couple. In such a climate of confrontation, the pastor gives precedence to the problems of marital fidelity and spiritual oneness; otherwise, to advise incompatible, childless couples to have a baby "is as unenlightened as it is dangerous. While it may succeed in holding a marriage together, who can say how many children are thus sacrificed on the altar of incompatibility."[3]

In summary, as the pastor corrects misconceptions and explores the emotional roots of self-diagnosis, he ministers to the couple's anxieties of grief, sin, finitude, inferiority and loneliness.

PASTORAL REASSURANCE

As infertile couples continue to communicate their problem, the pastor frequently observes that they are under a heavy emotional strain and that they are thus in need of reassurance which will enable them to face and to work through their problem.

Mrs. C felt guilty and unworthy of aid. She strongly resented, as personal betrayal, her husband's refusal to have a semen analysis. She confessed: "I hate to face anyone with my condition, especially an outsider," such as a medical specialist. Mr. C felt that he needed help from no one. He was proud of his "independence." He blamed his wife for their "tragedy" of sterility. At a loss as to what to do, yet feeling that he must do something, the pastor concluded the interview with a vague, generalized prayer that "God's will be done."

Vague generalities tend to depress rather than to support and are as inappropriate and inadequate for specific problems as a superficial physical examination concluded by advice to "take a couple of aspirins" and, by implication, to "leave it at that." To be effective,

[3] Morris Fishbein, *Children for the Childless. A Concise Explanation of the Medical, Scientific and Legal Facts about Conception, Fertility, Sterility, Heredity, and Adoption,* first edition (Garden City: Doubleday and Co., Inc.), p. 60.

pastoral reassurance must be specific and realistic in content and implication. To reassure Mrs. C effectively, for instance, the pastor should lead her to see the intrinsic worth of every person created in the image of God; whereas, her husband should be led to recognize human limitations and to feel unashamed that mutual dependence is needful. He supports the wife by informing her that, in reality, husbands are responsible for infertility in almost as many instances of childlessness as wives; thus, both the husband and the wife should accept responsibility for barrenness and be medically examined for infertility. The pastor realistically reassures them that knowing, rather than half-suspecting, even when sterility is absolute, is valuable toward making a new and healthier adjustment which is relieved of doubt and indecision. The pastor relieves their fear of the doctor's reaction by reassuring them that most doctors do not regard infertility as shameful, that physicians do not function in the judgmental role, that medical records are confidential and that the objective of the doctor is scientific accuracy and appropriate medical therapy.

ROLE AND FUNCTION OF THE PASTOR

Some pastors erroneously feel that the role and function of the minister indicates a hands-off policy toward the problem of sterility; and, if they have an unavoidable obligation, it is then restricted just to referral upon the direct request of the barren couple. For the many childless couples who interpret their problem as primarily theological in nature, however, the pastor is an appropriate and irreplaceable source of aid.

Although counseling the childless couple is a specialized problem in marriage and family counseling, the basic role and function of the pastor is not altered. In his relationship to the sterile couple, the pastor is to walk within his symbolic role of a representative, instrument and reminder of God and of a specific church. Despite the scope of his medical knowledge, the pastor does not symbolize medical authority to the counselee, and he is not expected to function in such a capacity. To do so is to encounter confusion, resentment and failure as a minister.

In keeping with the nature of God whom he represents, the pastor does not function to direct coercively the counselee's course of action. In a casual manner and as a matter of course, however, needful and timely questions which are restricted to relevant essentials are appropriate and helpful.

Infertility often results in serious domestic conflicts of assault upon the integrity of the spouse, private misunderstandings of resignation and loneliness, social involvement of infidelity and divorce. Marriage and family counseling is, therefore, a highly significant function in the pastoral care of the childless couple. As the pastor begins to counsel these couples, an appraisal of the personal resources of each spouse and of their interpersonal relationship is desirable, to determine the degree of marital disintegration and potential.

In contrast to the function of the physician who waits for persons to seek his assistance, a vital and unique function of the pastor is initiative. Distress, conflict, discomfort, inability to communicate and the various misconceptions which are frequent circumstances of the infertile couple indicate the need for pastoral initiative. The pastor will, however, be careful to leave the decision and responsibility to utilize the available sources of help, or the "psychological initiative," to the couple. Apart from pastoral initiative, the couple may lack both the information and the motivation for maximum fulfillment within their vocational calling of marriage.

In representing God, who maintains an unbroken covenant relationship with His own, and, in contrast to the physician whose aid terminates at the conclusion of diagnosis or treatment, the pastoral relationship is permanent. The pastor functions as an enduring spiritual guide, teacher and friend. In such a sense of Christian community with its reciprocal confidence and concern, strong relationships develop and serve as battering rams which penetrate otherwise impregnable barriers of the childless couple.

The complexity and dimensions of the infertility problem necessitate professional consultation. The pastor thus functions as a member of a "healing team" that is endeavoring to meet the total needs of the childless couple. No need exists for confusion or conflict among the professional roles, and care should be exercised lest boundaries, which limit the recognized roles and helpful functions of each, be violated. The minister may know a great deal about medicine, and the doctor may be able to deliver an edifying sermon, but, in counseling, the couple rightfully expects each to function without confusion in his recognized and accepted role.

REFERRAL

Although referral is indicated by the very nature of the infertility problem, this ministry is often resented and sometimes rejected outright until the prerequisite spiritual preparation is met. The pastor is thus cautioned against premature referral as well as solitary attempts to meet the total needs of the childless couple.

As the couple become spiritually prepared to consider the resources available to them for meeting their infertility needs, the pastor's task is the ministry of referral. This ministry includes information as to what help is available, where to go for help and the usual costs in time and money. The pastor is thus advised to acquaint himself with the family physicians, reputable gynecologists, urologists and psychiatrists, as well as with the facilities of the local hospitals, sterility clinics and adoption agencies. He should acquaint himself with pertinent literature on infertility and hand the couple appropriate reading material to implement their information.

Numerous couples do not know that anything can be done for them, and the informed pastor bears "good news" in his referral ministry.

> Mrs. T told her pastor that she did not know that she could be helped. She always felt that if you were to have a baby, then you would; otherwise, nothing could be done about it. The pastor informed her that an encouraging percentage of couples who received medical aid became parents. This information brought "tears of joy" to her eyes. She then wanted to know what doctor they should see and what he would do. The pastor referred her and her husband to their family physician, and informed them that he would probably refer them to competent specialists who would explain to them the physiology of reproduction, give them fertility tests, and recommend treatment if indicated by the diagnostic findings. Seeing no reason to consult their family physician, and desiring to save money, they asked for, and were furnished with, the names of reputable gynecologists and urologists in the area.

Although the average general practitioner is not qualified to diagnose sterility accurately, the family physician should know the developments of his patients. He is also in a better position than the pastor to make referrals to sterility specialists. By recalling these facts, the pastor wisely and indirectly discourages decisions to eliminate the family physician.

A host of childless couples have heard that help is available, but they have not taken advantage of their opportunities. Among this group are persons who do not associate their infertility with sinfulness, who have no definite conception of sterilty and who do not attempt self-diagnosis. At this point in counseling, such unbiased couples usually need only to be informed of the fundamentals of fertility and to be referred appropriately.

> Mr. and Mrs. P, ages 33 and 30, had been married for ten years, and for four years had sought unsuccessfully to have a child. Steadily the pressures within the couple increased with the passing of each of the years. One evening when the pastor "stopped by for a few minutes to say hello" they remarked on the birth of a child "next door," and stated that they "hoped and prayed" that they would be "next," and that they were "getting behind." Their pastor inquired as to their prayers concerning their childlessness, and asked if they felt that God was withholding parenthood from them for some reason. Mr. P replied, "We don't feel that God is punishing us. As a matter of fact, we feel that God is not taking a hand in this one way or the other . . . He's leaving it entirely to us." The pastor reflected, "Then, one possible explanation is ruled-out in your thinking." Mr. and Mrs. P nodded in affirmation. The pastor continued, "Am I correct in assuming that you have come to other definite conclusions about your childlessness?" "No," Mr. P replied, "it may have sounded that way, but we haven't. We've been thinking about seeing our doctor but . . . like a lot of things . . . we've kept putting it off. But we're not getting any younger, and we're going to have to do something about it soon or we'll be too old to start a family." Their pastor agreed with that conclusion, referred them to their family physician and orientated them in the fundamental facts of fertility so that they would have some idea of what to expect. He then concluded the interview with the request that he be kept informed of developments because he cared for them and their best welfare. One week later Mr. P called to tell his pastor that they had seen their family physician and that appointments with specialists for him and his wife had been made. He seemed glad that he had taken definite action and, accordingly, his pastor congratulated him.

As illustrated by Mr. and Mrs. P, the pastor performs a valuable service when he helps infertile couples to stop procrastinating, to come to wholesome decisions and to take definite action. Despite the fact that Mr. and Mrs. P stated that they had prayed about their problem, their pastor neglected to pray with them and, thereby, missed one of his strongest resources for reassurance in his referral ministry.

In anticipation of the couple's concern for costs in time and money of basic diagnostic tests, the pastor who secures this information beforehand from private physicians and from local clinics is to be commended. When such foresight is not exercised, then the next best thing is for the pastor to telephone for this information while the couple is still in the office and weighing the alternatives.

Comprehensive examinations necessitate a complete physical which includes x-rays, blood tests and urinalysis, in addition to the specific fertility tests of semen analysis of the husband and special gynecological tests of the wife. The rates of private physicians for diagnostic testing are usually higher than those of clinics. In several areas, a representative fee for private physicians is $50 each for the general physical and $25 each for the specialized fertility tests, a total of $150 for the couple. The same services at a local clinic are estimated at $110 total. Treatment, however, varies with the causes of infertility, and cannot generally be ascertained as to type, duration or costs prior to diagnosis.

A minimum of two office calls for the husband and three for the wife is usually required for diagnostic testing. The problem of costs in time may often be resolved by scheduling appointments on the couple's "days off" so that they will not have to be absent from work.

To be better informed and to have appropriate periodicals on hand to offer the sterile couple, the pastor can be supplied with excellent material from the Planned Parenthood Federation of America, the American Society for the Study of Sterility and the American Medical Society. Other helpful sources of information are the Maternity Health League and county medical societies (see Appendix C).

Before bidding the couple *bon voyage* on their advisable venture into a complete diagnostic survey, the pastor wisely takes the necessary steps to make sure that their hopes are realistic. The pastor is cautioned neither to state nor to leave the impression that all instances of infertility respond favorably to medical treatment. Currently, almost one-half of the seemingly infertile couples treated have had a child of their own; thus, on this factual basis, the pastor offers reassurance and realistic hope. The pastor should also assure the couple that, although he will not intrude into the realm of the doctor, he neither terminates his relationship nor considers their problem a "closed issue."

> After the appointments were made to see the medical specialists, Mr. T said, "Well, Brother W, you've done your part. I don't guess we'll be bothering you any more with our problem." The pastor assured them of his continuing concern, and stated that he would appreciate knowing the developments and their reactions to each development. Mr. and Mrs. T appreciated his concern, and promised to keep him informed. The religious resources of the Scriptures and of prayer were not used.

Scriptures offered on a prescription basis and prayers concerning specific needs are not and will never become outmoded in pastoral counseling at its best. The truly enlightened pastor will distinguish between the abuses and the abiding potential of these religious resources and, while avoiding their abuses, he will respect and use them properly. To eliminate the Scriptures and prayer on the misconception that better counseling results with their omission is to err gravely and to reduce drastically the effectiveness of pastoral counseling.

Such passages of Scripture as Genesis 30:14–17, in which Rachel sought and obtained mandrakes, may be interpreted to lend strong support for medical therapy. The pastor may further strengthen the couple's faith in the sanction of God upon their decision to seek medical aid by leading them in a prayer that the Creator will guide the physician and that He will bless every effort to cooperate with Him and His laws of nature. Such a prayer is, in the opinion of the writer, a most fitting benediction to the ministry of referral.

THREE

PASTORAL COUNSELING
DURING MEDICAL DIAGNOSIS

During the comprehensive medical survey, which usually requires two or three months for completion, tentative diagnosis and prognosis are withheld. This is a period of uncertainty, impatience and stress. Pastoral support is thus indicated to meet the needs of the couple for emotional release, information, reassurance and patience.

EMOTIONAL RELEASE

Emotional tension usually increases during the diagnostic survey and, unless released, the results can be disastrous. In one extreme situation, suicide was committed as the way of release from this period of tension. The trusted pastor should closely follow a couple's progress and encourage them to vent their feelings. He should, when necessary, take the initiative rather than risk letting their tension become acute. As the pastor affords a free, non-judicial, accepting and understanding atmosphere which respects the individual in his ability of self-direction, and as he leaves decision and direction to the counselee, the results to the counselee of self-expression are often cathartic, illuminating, incitive and supportive.

Three weeks after the appointment of Mr. and Mrs. T, their pastor had received no word from them. He telephoned. Mrs. T answered and said that she had intended to see him after receiving the medical report. She was very nervous, and desired to make an appointment with the pastor. That very evening both Mr. and Mrs. T came to the pastor's study. He counseled them separately. The pastor suggested to Mrs. T that she start anywhere she desired and completely "unwind." He listened prayerfully. She talked for thirty minutes without interruption, yet she was fully aware that her pastor was "with her" by the nodding of his head, his "hum-m-m" and his "um-hum." She then said, "Now that I've talked about it, it doesn't seem so bad. By explaining it to you, I understand it better myself." She laughed at herself and said, "It's wonderful to know that God is with me and helping me. Our being together tonight has helped me to realize it better than ever before." Previous counseling interviews had "set the stage" for these positive results.

In expressing their feelings and in explaining a problem there is cleansing release and illuminating insights which are supportive and essential to the pastoral care of the childless couple, and the emotional release has the added positive and desired results of being conducive to fertility.

The symbolic role of the pastor is an irreplaceable means of support. Merely by the pastor's presence and continuing concern, the childless couple often feel that both God and their pastor are with them and for them. This awareness relieves some of their loneliness.

Although the emotional stress of the husband during the diagnostic period is not usually as severe as that of the wife, he does experience stress and he is in need of pastoral support.

Mr. T expressed to the pastor his feelings of guilt and his difficulty of temporary impotency while masturbating in compliance with the semen analysis test. He stated that his seminal test was 40 percent, which was "low." He felt that the test was not representative, even though the doctor did not suggest that he repeat the test at a later date. He "felt wrong about the whole thing." The pastor suggested that he wait two or three months, build himself up, and repeat the test. He assured Mr. T that masturbation for the purpose of seminal tests was ethically comparable to other laboratory tests, such as blood tests and urinalysis, and, therefore, not sinful. Mr. T then stated that he felt "very much relieved." They prayed for God's guidance as Mr. T sought to achieve maximum general health and higher fertility prior to making an appointment for a second seminal test.

Interpretations of masturbation run the gauntlet from the strictest puritanism to a psychological factor only which is void of ethical significance. The pastor may have very definite and strong convictions on the subject, but to further his ethical position is primarily a pulpit rather than a counseling ministry. The counselor may sometimes help the couple by stating his beliefs, as, for example, did Mr. T's pastor, but to press for conformity to his concepts may further complicate rather than resolve the problems of the barren.

INFORMATION

The pastor may support childless couples by reaffirming the necessity for comprehensive testing for accurate diagnosis. The husband whose first seminal test is substandard may be reassured that, in current practice, more than one analysis is made before the diagnosis is credited. By such appropriate dissemination of factual information the couple receive support and strength to renew their efforts.

While masturbation for purposes of fertility testing is opposed by Roman Catholics, supported by most Protestants and questioned by Jews, there are those within each faith who conscientiously differ with prevailing beliefs of their particular religious denomination. Rather than to anticipate on the basis of commonly held positions, the need to approach this problem on an individual basis is indicated. Objections to masturbation for diagnostic testing is usually both an emotional and an ethical problem. If, for any reason, infertile husbands object to such tests, they may be greatly relieved to know that they have the alternative of a post-coital examination of the wife.

Some husbands, who state that they have no moral objections to masturbation for the seminal test, react with feelings of guilt after these tests.

"When I was a child," Mr. O said, "I got some hard whippings for playing with myself. Mother shamed me and made me feel terribly low-down and dirty. I remember one time when I had done it again. . . . Mother was so aggravated with me that she got the butcher knife. She made me take down my pants, then she got a hold of it and asked me if she was going to have to cut it off to make me stop. Well, I'll never forget that! (Long pause). When Dad heard about it, he just laughed and said to me, 'Boy, you'd better leave that thing alone. When you get bigger we'll talk about this again.' (Another long pause, the pastor waiting quietly and patiently.) "I can't see anything wrong with doing the test," Mr. O continued, "but I feel wrong about it. You know . . . I looked up the word 'masturbation' in the dictionary one time and found that it was called 'self-abuse.' Well, if it's abuse, then it seems to me that it's a 'waste' no matter how good the reason to do it. I don't know . . . do you?" The pastor reflected, "This has been a major problem that has troubled you for a long time, hasn't it?" Mr. O replied, "That's right."

The pastor said, "Mr. O, let me ask you this; do you feel the least bit wrong in any way about having sexual relations with your wife?" Mr. O answered, "No . . . no, that's not true. Sometime when I use prevention to keep from having a baby I feel that I'm 'wasting' my 'seed' and this doesn't seem right . . . it's sorta like I'm trying to go against my Maker." The pastor, venturing an association, said, "Is this feeling of 'waste' like your feelings about masturbation?" "I'd never thought of the two together before, but they are a lot alike. Do they have a connection?" Mr. O queried. The pastor responded, "Maybe, but you'd be in a better position to answer that than I would." Mr. O asked, "How can I find out?" The pastor answered his question with a question, "Would you like to talk about these feelings, beginning at the time when they first started bothering you and coming on to the present? It will take time, but it could answer several problems." Mr. O said that he would "like that very much," and once per week interviews for two months were scheduled.

The pastor then explained post-coital testing to him and Mr. O was quite relieved when informed of this alternative; then, just as the pastor was about to end the interview, Mr. O said, "I've got one more question I want to ask you before we go. Do you think that I harmed myself by playing with myself when I was a boy? We've tried, many times we've tried, but my wife and I still haven't gotten a baby yet, and I've wondered about it a lot of times." The pastor replied, "It's not likely. Ask your doctor, and when he tells you that this didn't make you barren, then you'll know for sure and feel better." Mr. O came back quickly, "I don't want to ask him anything like that!" The pastor then informed him that his doctor would think nothing of it and would be happy to relieve his mind on that subject. The interview was then terminated by a confirmation of the time of their next appointment for counseling.

Many unresolved problems associated with sex may be uncovered, resurrected, and pushed to the forefront during the period of comprehensive medical testing for an accurate diagnosis. The pastor may thus be confronted with a host of complex emotional problems, such as ambivalence, inordinate feelings of guilt and a castration "complex." When such negative emotions persist, pastoral counseling over an extended period of time in a controlled relationship, referral for psychotherapy or both may be indicated to reach the emotional roots of the problem.

REASSURANCE

Infertile women who object to some of the fertility tests, such as the post-coital examination, need pastoral reassurance.

> Mrs. T was told by her doctor to report to his office thirty minutes after coitus for a post-coital test. She objected, and told her pastor that she didn't feel right about getting up from the bed and going straight to the doctor. "He would know we had just finished 'making love,' and I wouldn't feel right about seeing him for that test." Despite her pastor's comments that the doctor knew already, and that the test was quite helpful to establish accurate diagnosis, she steadfastly refused the test, and would have discontinued all examinations had the test been mandatory. Instead of continuing to approach an emotional problem on an intellectual basis, the pastor then reassured Mrs. T that the diagnostic survey should be continued, and the stronger emotion prevailed. Upon consulting the doctor, they learned that other tests could be substituted and, though less effective, her examination was continued on that basis.

The need for perseverance and cooperation to obtain a correct diagnosis is essential, and the pastor may support the couple by recalling to mind their objective of doing everything within their power that is not morally wrong to bring about conception. When faced with emotional blockage, such as that of Mrs. T, however, the pastor's task is to inform such persons of the alternatives of testing and to reassure them that the diagnostic survey should be completed.

To further support and strengthen the couple, the pastor may reaffirm his faith in his medical referral by explicit statements of confidence in the diagnostic efforts of the doctor and by confirming with them their experience of something gained, yet nothing lost, within the relationships of pastor, doctor and self.

PATIENCE

Prolonged waiting when fulfillment of the heart's desire is assured tries one's patience and, when childless couples do not know whether or not their time, efforts and money are invested "in vain," the stress on patience is often distressing.

Mrs. O said to her pastor, "This waiting is killing me. When I see a baby I want to shout for joy over the prospect of having one of my own; then I want to cry when I think that it may never be. Day after day, and still no news! Every day my nerves are wound up one turn tighter. We aren't rich either, as you know, and we have a very busy schedule. If we don't have a baby after all this, we've sacrificed a lot for nothing. I can't take much more of this waiting. My patience is at the breaking point now." The pastor asked, "What is the immediate goal of diagnosis?" Mrs. O answered, "To find out what's wrong so that we can have a baby." The pastor then showed her that she was expecting diagnosis to include treatment and prognosis, three goals which are distinct, needful and consecutive steps toward fertility. He informed Mrs. O that learning the facts only is the object of diagnosis, and that goal would, in all probability, be achieved. He then quoted John 8:32, "And ye shall know the truth, and the truth shall make you free." He interpreted this Scripture to show the value of diagnosis which frees them from wondering anxiously and imagining wildly as to "why" they can not have a baby. He counseled that she take "one step at a time," as they come with the dawn of each new day.

In addition to John 8:32, patience may be furthered in counseling by reading and interpreting to the barren couple such passages of Scripture as Psalm 69:1–8, Isaiah 40:28–31, Matthew 6:27–34, Romans 5:1–8, 8:24–39 and James 1:3–4.

Couples who are discouraged by the strangeness and complexity of the fertility investigation may be informed by their pastor that in the very complexity of the situation there are more alternatives for hope.

Failing to understand infertility, its therapy, and its "fifty-fifty" chances of favorable prognosis, some couples "give up" prematurely. Since fertility testing is based upon valid experience with the biological laws of cause and effect, the pastor may, therefore, appropriately reassure the couple that the examinations and therapies are not "hit or miss" endeavors. The pastor may furnish the couple with added stimuli to continue the fertility examination by leading them to consider the alternatives of possible conception and adoption. As he compares these alternatives, the pastor may remind the couple of the prolonged time factor of each. The comparison supports continued efforts toward conception and encourages a renewed determination to complete the fertility testing.

USE OF RELIGIOUS RESOURCES

The pastor's most powerful means of support, however, is the use of religious resources, especially those of the Bible and of prayer. Since the probability of their use is unlikely by one other than a minister, the pastor should not neglect so great a responsibility and opportunity as a steward of these resources.

The pastor may interpret Genesis 18:9–15, 25:21 and 30:1–24, Scriptures which refer to the barrenness of Sarah, Rebekah and Rachel, to indicate that sterility, with all its frustrations, may serve to test faith and patience. For those who are in covenant relationship with God, this can be a valuable discipline.

As the couple proceed into the diagnostic period, the pastor may interpret Genesis 30:14, Psalm 37:4–7, Mark 2:17 and Galatians 6:9 to reaffirm and to strengthen their faith in the procedure which they have begun. Ecclesiastes 3:1, Matthew 24:13, Luke 8:15, 18:1, Romans 5:3–4, 8:25, 12:12, 15:4–5, James 1:2–4, 2 Peter 1:5–8 and portions of Psalms 27, 40, 46, 103, 118 and 127 may serve to renew their strength so that they will steadfastly and patiently persevere through these trying experiences, and will be saved from failing to meet their personal responsibilities in effecting conception.

Romans 12:1 and 1 Corinthians 9:24–25 may strengthen the couple to change their daily habits to those which are conducive to increased fertility through maximum general health.

Each clinical situation conditions the appropriateness of a given Scripture. Passages of Scripture which are carefully selected, timely used and firmly believed may witness frustrations resolved, disillusionments enlightened, fears dispelled and conscience healed.

To lead the couple to direct contact with the Author of life through the religious resource of prayer is a paramount privilege and responsibility of the pastor. The power of prayer is illustrated in I Samuel 1:9–20, and, as circumstances permit identification with Hannah and Eli, childless couples are aided to the incomparable resource of effectual prayer.

Prayers, such as those found in portions of Psalms 25, 31, 42, 51, 63, 71, 123, 130 and 139, are pointedly applicable and highly supportive to many couples in this developmental stage of their sterility problem. To lead these couples to make such prayers their own is a pastoral function which approaches the apex of strength.

On the basis of these supportive Scriptures, the pastor finds words to strengthen his intercessory prayers. Although the pastor should adapt his prayer to the specific need of each situation, the following prayer may suggest to him a few of the multiple possibilities in Scripturally-based, intercessory prayer.

> O God, our help in ages past, our hope for years to come, Thou art a very present help in trouble. For Thy bountiful grace and abiding love we are grateful. These Thy children, in committing their ways unto Thee, have felt, as did Rachel of old, Thy leadership in seeking aid to fertility. Lest impatience lead them to shrink from following after Thee, grant unto them firmness of purpose like that of our Lord Jesus Christ as He steadfastly set His face to go to Jerusalem and would not be dissuaded. Lest they lose heart and fail to reap the fruit of persevering cooperation with Thee, strengthen their faith as they patiently pursue and responsibly discharge their stewardship obligations under Thee, the Creator of life. Amen.

Abstract platitudes disqualify as supportive prayer; whereas, logical, realistic and spiritually mature prayer, which is in keeping with the character of God, avails much toward supplying the childless couple with needful strength.

Until the couple clearly and realistically see their physical limitations and potentialities, the pastor appropriately teaches them to pray, in faith and in submission to God's sovereignty, "Lord, what wouldst thou have me to do?" This helps the person to find God and to discover the physical, mental and emotional dimensions of himself. Upon finding God and upon acquiring self-knowledge, the pastor logically leads the couple to pray, in complete dedication to the specific leadership of God, "Thy will be done," and thus to accept themselves within their fences of human frailties and of individual variations (Deuteronomy 4:29 and Luke 22:42).

Within the will of God, which may either include or exclude the vocation of parenthood, the pastor appropriately seeks to lead the childless couple from self-centeredness to Christ-centeredness and, thereby, to fulfillment of life. Since, despite limitations and childlessness, abundant life is possible in Christ, the pastor offers hope and teaches the couple to offer a benedictory prayer of praise to God in whom life is victorious (Matthew 10:37–39).

These examples of prayer are for the purpose of suggesting to the pastor the dynamic place of prayer in counseling the childless couple.

Of the many means of pastoral support, not all are timely in a given situation. Each clinical situation conditions the appropriateness of a given means of support; hence, for maximum support and reasurrance, the pastor, as the physician of the soul, counsels the childless couple on a prescription basis only.

FOUR

Upon DISCOVERING
The CAUSE Of STERILITY

CAUSES OF STERILITY

The causes of sterility are highly significant to the pastoral care of the infertile couple because they affect emotional response and condition treatment.

In conference with the doctor after completion of the diagnostic survey, the couple learn the causes of their infertility, the recommended treatment as applicable, and their probable prognosis. To prevent adverse reactions from becoming advanced, and to further the development of wholesome concepts and sound attitudes toward their limitations, the pastor seeks an interview with the couple as soon as practicable after they learn the results of their fertility examination.

The three broad categories of sterility are organic, psychic and a combination of the two. Within these broad categories, the causal factors of infertility may be classified as general, male, female, environmental, voluntary, emotional and unknown.

General. Any condition that impairs healthy functioning of the body decreases fertility. Several conditions which impair general health and which receive repeated emphasis by medical authorities include malnutrition, obesity, insufficient rest, glandular disturbances, improper exercise, constitutional diseases, focal infections, blood incompatibilities, anemia, tuberculosis, gonorrhea, syphilis, irritating contraceptives, older age, duration of sterility, heredity, excessive use of tobacco, alcohol or drugs, septic tonsils, prolonged work, poisoning from decayed teeth, improper development of sex organs and hormonal deficiencies or excesses. Accordingly, the pastor appropriately emphasizes the importance of the couple's responsibility to God of preserving and enhancing general health (Romans 12:1 and 1 Corinthians 6:19–20).

The busy schedule of Mr. J, a 38-year-old executive, permitted him only five hours sleep per night, and prevented him from eating regularly. He was, however, constantly nibbling on "sweets" and pastries. He became obese. He did not exercise. He was emotionally tense, and he drank and smoked excessively. The pastor confronted him with his stewardship responsibilities in physical health, and Mr. J admitted that he was doing wrong, but he also stated that he could see "no way out." The pastor suggested several alternatives, including a change in vocations. Mr. J later changed his vocation, increasingly conformed to the biological laws of nature, and reaped steadily improved general health.

While a direct statement by the pastor as to what the couple "ought to do" may be well received as, for example, in the case of Mr. J, the results are usually far better when the pastor leads the couple to perceive and to voice their own convictions of personal obligation.

Prior to penicillin and other antibiotics, an estimated 50 percent of all sterile marriages resulted from gonorrhea or syphilis and gonorrhea combined accounted for more cases of sterility than all other diseases combined. Currently, however, the percentage has declined considerably due to these antibiotics; but these diseases are not eliminated because some of the many who are promiscuous either do not secure these prophylactics or procrastinate too long before taking preventive measures.

Since venereal diseases are most frequently transmitted through illicit sexual intercourse, when sterility is the result of these diseases the pastor is usually dealing with overt sin and actual guilt (1 Corinthians 6:13–18); hence venereal diseases add an ethical and moral dimension to the problem of infertility which merits special attention of the pastor.

Religious persons who know that their sterility is caused by venereal diseases usually suffer acute feelings of guilt. The pastor's task is to lead such persons to reconciliation to God, which involves a conviction and cleansing from sin through godly grief, repentance and commitment to right paths. In the Spirit of the Lord, the pastor does not condemn. He urges them to go their way and sin no more, lest something worse befall them (2 Corinthians 7:10; John 5:14, and John 8:11).

Sterility as a result of venereal diseases often brings marital conflict. To forgive the "offending" person may be extremely difficult, especially for the fertile mate who intensely desires children. After the couple have vented such feelings and voiced their opinions, the pastor may promote forgiveness and reconciliation by linking the Scriptural position of Matthew 6:14–15 with the example of the forgiving Christ and with a reminder of the basic unitive purpose of marriage between two persons who are bound together in love.

> Mr. M, age 22, while in the military service in Korea, contracted gonorrhea. In pre-marital counseling with his chaplain he asked if he should confess to his fiancee. He stated that the doctor said that he was all "cleared up" and that he would not transmit a disease to his bride. He and the chaplain came to the conclusion that future fidelity was essential, and that confession to God only was necessary. Mr. M was married the following year. Two years thereafter, they sought fertility testing. The results showed that Mrs. M was fertile, and that Mr. M was sterilized by gonorrhea. Mrs. M, greatly disturbed, left him to "spend a few days" with her parents. She felt that she had been deceived. Mr. M brought his problem to his pastor. He felt extremely guilty. He revealed his sins to his pastor and, upon the pastor's suggestion, prayed for forgiveness. Mr. M committed his future to God. The pastor contacted Mrs. M, and an appointment was made for an interview. The pastor explained to her that Mr. M had entered marriage believing that nothing was wrong with him, that he did not deliberately deceive her and that he affirmed his fidelity in marriage. The pastor asked Mrs. M if she could accept his infertility had the cause been other than venereal disease, and she said that she could, but that it would "still hurt." After two interviews with each separately and one with them together, the pastor succeeded in "getting them back together," but their relationship continued to be "strained." The pastor neither referred them to a psychiatrist nor sought to counsel them on a long-term basis. Having done all he knew to do, he dropped the problem.

As the pastor learns in pre-marital counseling that a person has a medical history of venereal disease, he wisely leads the person to see the need for fertility testing. Should the person reject this referral, the task of the pastor is to inform the counselee of his moral obligation to tell his fiancee of his possible infertility.

The emotional reaction to sterilization by gonorrhea is extremely intense for both husband and wife. The need for pastoral counseling on a long-term basis in a controlled relationship is indicated to bring the couple to mutual understanding and forgiveness, to reconciliation and marital harmony.

Until the problem of the couple is resolved, the pastor has, despite his limitations, a ministry to perform. While maintaining a sustained relationship, he can and should refer the couple, as indicated, to a doctor, psychiatrist, social worker, or fellow minister whose clinical training and experience qualify him for the referral.

Male. Currently, the husband is infertile in almost as many instances of childlessness as the wife. This is due to azoospermia or no sperm, faulty spermatogenesis or "weak" sperm, and faulty transmission of spermatozoa or improper passage of sperm.

Ten causes of male infertility are (1) complications from previous diseases, such as mumps, gonorrhea, typhoid fever, syphilis and tuberculosis; (2) endocrine disturbance, such as those affecting the pituitary, thyroid and adrenal glands; (3) injuries to testes or genital tract; (4) spermatic exhaustion from excessive coitus or masturbation; (5) chronic intoxicants, such as alcoholism, drug addiction or metallic poisons; (6) undescended testicles; (7) pseudo-sterility, or psychic or constitutional impotency; (8) congestions or varicosities; (9) extreme external heat, and (10) constitutional inferiority such as general debility, insanity, avitaminosis and hereditary defects.[1]

Approximately 61 percent of the male alcoholics are impotent and thus pseudo-sterile. From biological necessity as well as from an ethical perspective, the resolution of the alcohol problem takes precedence over the sterility problem.

Mr. L, age 36, after eight years of marriage, sought tests for fertility. His seminal test was quantitatively "low," but qualitatively "good." The doctor advised him to stop drinking. Disturbed by his seminal deficiency and by his business reversals, he increased his drinking. He became impotent. His wife "left him." He then sought help from his pastor. After three interviews with each, they again "lived under the same roof," but they were far from united. The non-judgmental pastor sought first to understand Mr. L, and to help him to find the solution to his alcohol problem. The pastor explored his religious background and felt that, although Mr. L was a church member, he had not been "converted." On the fourth interview, Mr. L "accepted

[1] Abner I. Weisman, *Spermatozoa and Sterility: A Clinical Manual* (New York: Hoeber Medical Div., Harper & Row, Publishers, 1941), pp. 38–40, 219–23.

Christ." He came to church and professed his faith. The pastor helped him to find a less strenuous vocation. Mr. L stopped drinking and joined the local chapter of Alcoholics Anonymous. His potency was restored. The pastor counseled Mr. and Mrs. L for several interviews. The barriers to communication began to fall, and marital harmony increased. They then turned their attention to the problem of sterility. A subsequent examination of Mr. L revealed that his seminal test was 45 percent, a slightly higher percentage than his initial test.

Since alcoholism is a physical and emotional sickness, the pastor whose approach is non-judgmental is far more helpful to the alcoholic than those who regard the alcohol problem as merely a matter of "willpower." Prior to ministering to the sterility problems of such couples as Mr. and Mrs. L, the pastor should, therefore, lead them to the resolution of their alcohol problem, and should promote marital harmony.

Some infertile men worry about the effect of frequency of coitus upon their fertility. The pastor can help to relieve this worry by informing them that medical authorities generally agree that the sperm value is inadequate when the frequency is of less than 24 hour intervals, but that a 48 hour interval is usually sufficient for full sperm value. Intervals which extend for several days or weeks usually result in less active and faulty sperm rather than in more and better sperm.

The pastor may frequently encounter bitter remorse in the person who is involuntarily sterilized, or emasculated, by force or by accident.

Mr. Q, age 25, became sterile as a result of injuries to his testicles which he received when thrown from his motorcycle onto a fence. For months after he was able to return to work, he remained idle. Despite the efforts of his pastor, he refused to acknowledge his condition. He did not mourn, and he was not comforted. He became bitter toward "fate" and the church. He became hypercritical, and he developed a "temper" with a "very low boiling point." The pastor then sought to "rehabilitate" him through contacts with the young men and women of the church. Mr. Q became "interested" in a young war widow who had three children, and who was quite active in the church. Two years later, Mr. Q married her and, in the loving acceptance of his wife and her children, he came to be reconciled to God, the church and himself.

Some involuntarily sterilized persons may reject the pastor and his referral ministry. By assuring them of the continuing availability of his ministry and, indirectly, by enlisting the services of others in the church who can establish a positive relationship with them, the pastor ministers to their needs.

Female.   A prevalent cause of female infertility is the obstruction of the genital tract. The Fallopian tubes or the cervix, for instance, may be blocked by local infections or by other obstructive congestions.

Common causes of female infertility are dysmenorrhea, endometriosis, endocrine disturbance, irregular menses, over or under secretion and post-coital douching. The Scriptures accurately describe female sterility as a "closed womb" (I Samuel 1:5–6).

A basic cause of female sterility is failure of ovulation. There must be a fertilizable ovum or egg. No ovum means no baby, even when all other factors are right.

Impairment or loss of fertility in women may be associated with a host of diseases, conditions or factors. Surgical and endocrine factors, any congenital disturbance, acute appendicitis, frigidity which repels coitus, older age, acute conditions or infectious diseases and chronic debilitating states are but a few of the many things which can prevent pregnancy. An equally large number of associated factors are operative during pregnancy, as is attested by the one of every four pregnancies which terminate in abortion, miscarriage or stillbirth.

The loss of fertility usually brings intense grief to the sterile wife. She is in a bereavement crisis which indicates the urgency of her need and the appropriateness of pastoral counseling.

Mrs. T was informed by her gynecologist that she had acute endometriosis, and that she would probably never have a baby. She was so shocked that she spent about six hours sitting and staring into space. When Mr. T came home from work that evening, she told him what the doctor said, burst into tears and cried most of the night. The next day she was deeply depressed. She felt that she was guilty of failing her husband by being unable to give him a child. Coupled with feelings of inferiority, she became increasingly depressed. Mr. T's efforts to reassure her of his love produced a fresh outburst of tears and increased depression. He then called their pastor and explained her situation. The pastor came immediately. Mr. T strongly believed that God would yet give them a child. The pastor urged Mrs. T to "talk about it." She talked for over an hour, "poured out" her heart of everything, including her hopes, plans and dreams for her children-to-be in each phase of growth. She mourned her loss as though a live, healthy baby had died in her arms. Only then did the pastor speak words of sympathy and hope. The pastor then reminded her that her prognosis for pregnancy was not completely void of hope, even though everything humanly possible had been done. With a conscience clear of personal responsibilities for infertility, both the husband and the wife prayed, and left the entire problem in the "hands of God." They said, in effect, "Nevertheless, not my will but thine be done." They decided against conscious efforts to time the ovulation cycle and for sexual relations apart from conception considerations. Four months later, Mr. and Mrs. T visited their pastor and shared the joyous news of her pregnancy. The pastor led them in a prayer of thanksgiving and praise to God. Their sterility problem was resolved, and nine months later they became the "proud parents" of a healthy, normal baby girl.

The understanding pastor helps childless couples to mourn, and to vent their feelings of guilt, hostility and inferiority. He seeks to lead them to attitudes which acknowledge the sovereignty of God and realistically accept personal limitations (Proverbs 28:13; Matthew 5:3–11; and James 5:16). As the couple meet the human element of responsibility toward effecting pregnancy, the pastor seeks to lead them to make peace with divine providence, to trust in God submissively and to come to pray, "Thy will be done," and, "The Lord gave, and the Lord has taken away; blessed be the name of the Lord" (Job 1:21 RSV; Matthew 26:42).

Had Mrs. T been diagnosed as hopelessly sterile, the pastor would not be in a position to offer hope for pregnancy. His initial ministry to bereavement would, otherwise, be essentially the same. After the bereavement crisis, he may appropriately explore with the hopelessly barren couple the alternative of adoption.

Although infertility as the result of induced abortion is not, in the strictest sense, classified as primary sterility, it is primary to the union within which conception has never occurred and, thus interpreted, induced abortion comes within the scope of this writing.

Induced abortion most frequently occurs in unwed women and usually results in permanent sterility. When the sterility of the wife is the result of induced abortion, she finds the crushing weight of constant guilt feelings almost more than she can bear. She not only is ever conscious of being deprived of children but also is hostile toward men, and especially toward the man who "got her in trouble."

> Miss S, age 18, became pregnant by her boy friend. They then "broke up." She left home when she was three months pregnant, and she secretly obtained "help" to abort. She came home one year later, confessed before her pastor and "rededicated" her life in church the following Sunday. She found a new boy friend, and was married to him six months later. At the time, neither her husband nor her pastor knew that she was sterile. Two years later, a competent diagnostic survey revealed her condition of sterility, which was caused by gynecological complications from induced abortion. She became deeply depressed. Her husband brought her to her former pastor. She admitted doing wrong, and prayed for forgiveness, but she would neither accept forgiveness nor be reconciled to her condition. Her depression increased to the point of attempted suicides. Psychiatric help was sought and, together with pastoral counseling by the pastors of the husband and of the wife, she approached the "norm." Currently, she seems to "tolerate" her childlessness, but she seems not to be reconciled to God, to herself, or to the "boy friend" who was "responsible." She "pets" her husband but, despite her compensatory deeds, she feels that she can not "make up" for denying him of children. Her husband loves her, and hopes that they can adopt children. In the durable relationships of her pastor and of her husband, a positive solution to her problem may yet be achieved.

The Christian pastor is ethically obligated to support civil law which contends that the fetus is a person and that induced abortion is "criminal." The only legitimate reason for induced abortion is self-preservation in which the alternative is either abortion or death of the pregnant woman. By the use of the Scriptures, such as Proverbs 28:13, and by illustrations which show the harmful effects of concealed abortion, the pastor may further confession and repentance. As the pastor expresses and demonstrates an understanding and forgiving attitude, he, without compromising his ethical stand against abortion, makes himself immediately accessible to those who commit this "crime."

In other instances of induced abortion, prideful parents pressure the unwed mother both to leave the community and to secure an abortion.

Mr. M, age 19, a pampered son of a prominent and prosperous family, "fell in love" with Miss W, age 17, of the same upperclass social bracket. The fathers of Mr. M and Miss W met and, to "avoid a public scandal," arranged to send the girl away for an abortion under the pretext of sending her to a private school. Both Mr. M and Miss W affirmed their love for each other, their desire to keep the baby and their desire to be married immediately even if it meant elopement to avoid the more serious blight upon the family name of illegitimacy. Threats to "cut them off" completely, however, prevailed. Two years after the abortion Miss W returned to her home, and she and Mr. M were formally wed in an extravagant church wedding. The couple began immediate efforts to have a baby to replace the one they "lost." One year later their desires for a baby were so desperate that they dared to seek help and to risk any possible stigma which it might bring upon them and their families. They sought medical aid, and the diagnostic findings revealed that the wife was permanently sterile as a result of her induced abortion; then, as a last resort, they came to their pastor, revealed their plight, and asked, "What shall we do?" The pastor heard their confession, prayed with them and suggested that they "start anew" with God. He later suggested the alternative of adoption. Mrs. M, in tearful anguish, said, "I don't deserve to have a baby . . . ever! And (looking at her husband), neither do you!" Further interviews were arranged, and as the guilt was seen corporately rather than individually, the couple's tension decreased, and they began to consider the "new start" which the pastor mentioned earlier, and the possibility of adopting a baby.

While the pastor does not attempt to justify unwed mothers for their illicit "love" and their subsequent abortion, neither does he desire that they unjustly assume the total burden of guilt. In most instances, a society comprised of parents, friends, neighbors and fellow members of various organizations are more responsible for this evil, and their role in this problem needs to be exposed repeatedly until they come to hang their heads in shame rather than to sniff in haughty scorn.

In counseling childless couples, the pastor often finds that social salvation to new and hopeful relationships may be, as in the instance of Mr. and Mrs. M, prerequisite to their consideration of spiritual salvation.

The problem of sterility, as in the case of Mr. and Mrs. M, is frequently so advanced by the time the couple come to their pastor that the choices are limited to mitigation and control rather than "cure." Before the pastor can help many such couples through a preventive ministry, the public will have to be re-educated to their "corporate responsibility" for youth in trouble.

Women who are sterile from induced abortion are often keenly conscious of their sin, and are heavily burdened with guilt. The pastor should not deepen their wounds of sin and guilt. He should, instead, lead them to repent, to accept forgiveness and to reconciliation to God. To overcome their darkness of despair which views life as a total loss, the pastor seeks to give them a hopeful vision of possible achievement in God in whom life is supremely worthwhile. A literal interpretation of Matthew 5:29–30, for example, offers one basis for realistic hope.

When confession and prayer bring no cleansing relief, and when depression is progressive, the pastor should insist on psychiatric assistance, lest the "sickness" from induced abortion be unto death by suicide (2 Corinthians 7:10).

Environmental. Environmental factors, such as climate, occupation and residence, can cause infertility. As we have already noted, high altitudes for the unacclimated and high environmental temperature may produce infertility. As the doctor recommends a change in residence, for example, to a climate that is cooler and less humid, the pastor's task is to help the couple to weigh the relative values of their present location and occupation with those of the recommended changes which may enhance, but not insure, conception.

> Mr. and Mrs. A were advised to move from the hot, humid climate of lower Louisiana to a dry and cooler climate. They discussed it, "pro and con," with their pastor, and elected to move. Mr. A managed to be transferred to another branch of the same company in a semi-mountainous region of Tennessee. The only apparent variable was the environmental factor. One year later Mrs. A conceived.

The pastor's task in counseling the childless couple concerning a change of residence to a more favorable climate is to help them to see and to weigh all of the assets and liabilities of the proposed change. The pastor is not to make the decision for them. Together with the doctor, the pastor realistically reminds the couple that not all have the happy results as did Mr. and Mrs. A.

Many occupations impair or prevent fertility. Employment in tobacco industries, for instance, irritate the genital tract of some women and prevent fertility. Occupations that are fatiguing, sedentary employment, industrial poisoning from exposure to gasoline, benzine or heavy metal fumes, over-exposure to radiation and work in extremely hot engine rooms adversely affect fertility.

When the doctor recommends a change in vocation due to such factors as over-fatigue or industrial poisoning, the pastor weighs with the infertile laborer his vocational aptitudes, the availability of work which he is qualified to perform and the probable economic security of the vocation. The pastor may further help such persons to make the needful occupational change by commending them to prospective employers.

From a fertility perspective, "rural life" is far better than "city life." Although those in rural areas have a 63 percent higher fertility rate than those in urban areas, a change of residence is not necessarily indicated, but a decrease in emotional tension is. The sensible pastor is certainly not going to advocate a mass exodus of sterile couples to the country, but, he can most assuredly advocate that the urban childless couple pattern their pace by the fertile and typical rural resident.

Voluntary.   The voluntary factor in sterility usually involves sterilization for preventive, protective, eugenic and health purposes. Some persons are medically advised to undergo sterilization in such situations as degenerative and disabling diseases, familial type feeblemindedness, manic-depressive psychosis, schizophrenia, leprosy or epilepsy. Sterilization is of two types, permanent and restorative, but the prognosis for reversing sterilization is poor. When the health of the mother is such that a pregnancy would endanger her life, and when the birth of "normal," healthy children cannot be expected, sterilization is medically advised.

As the doctor advises persons to undergo sterilization due to such factors as degenerative diseases or familial type feeble-mindedness, the pastor is confronted with the ethic of voluntary sterilization. When the life of the wife is at stake, the basic ethical issue becomes,

"Should a cherished person's life be gambled for the prospects of an infant of unknown quality?"

Mr. U was informed by his doctor that pregnancy would probably prove fatal to his wife who had developed "heart trouble." The doctor recommended that Mr. U be sterilized by vasectomy, rather than to risk control by contraceptives. Mr. U sought his pastor's advice on the ethics of such action, expressed his sorrow that pregnancy would not be possible, and feared that his virility would be affected by sterilization. The pastor supported both the doctor's advice that he be sterilized to save Mrs. U's life and the doctor's reassurance that sterilization does not affect virility. Believing that the basic unitive purpose in marriage was fulfilled, and that conception would result in the death of Mrs. U, the pastor stated that sterilization seemed ethically obligatory. The pastor led Mr. U to express his grief; then he read Psalm 46 and Philippians 4, and prayed that the couple find, and adjust well in, their vocational calling. Experience subsequent to his vasectomy verified his virility. The pastor maintained a permanent relationship with the couple. Mr. U came to discuss the subject freely, and even with a touch of humor. The couple now own and operate a large hardware store, and they happily act as though they were foster parents of all the neighborhood children.

The Scriptures may be interpreted to lend moral support of sterilization not only to preserve life but also, in some instances, to enhance life (Matthew 5:29-30; Isaiah 56:3-5; Jeremiah 38:7-13, and Matthew 19:12).

Despite the fact that sterilization of the husband by vasectomy is, by far, a more simple procedure than sterilization of the wife by hysterectomy, removal of ovaries, or tying of the "tubes," most husbands insist that their wives, rather than themselves, undergo the indicated surgery. In some instances, however, such as the case of Mrs. U, the wife's life would be endangered by major surgery; thus the husband must assume that responsibility which cannot be delegated to the wife. The pastor renders a valuable service to the couple as he helps the husband to see and to accept readily his responsibility in preserving and enhancing the life of his wife. The husband who can identify with Mr. U and adjust as he did is to be commended.

When a healthy child cannot be expected, the pastor not only should seriously question the ethical right of the couple to parenthood, but also should lead them to avoid conception voluntarily.

A missionary to a leper colony related that the law required sterilization as a prerequisite to marriage for persons with leprosy. He supported the law and officiated in these marriages. He interpreted the
will of God as opposing the furtherance of eugenic defects, such as
leprosy, through procreation. Many of the lepers were "in love," and
Rev. R felt that marital unity should not be withheld from them.

The ethical concepts of the pastor to Mr. U and of the missionary to the leper colony in China offer a wholesome Christian approach to the specific moral issue of sterilization. On the same ethical
basis, the chaplain of a state hospital should support sterilization of
mental defectives and sociopathological persons who cannot control
their sexual instincts. The chaplain has the cooperation and support
of most of these patients and their relatives in this means of rehabili-
tation, and the prognosis of such sterilized persons for positive adjustment to marriage and to community life is "good."

Emotional.   The first and second most frequent causes of
psychogenic sterility are unconscious fear and conscious or unconscious chronic anxieties. Emotional immaturity, rejection of parental
roles, repressions, intense hostilities, severe shock or excitement, unresolved Oedipal situations, coitus on command, amotiveness, exag-
gerations of "integrity" and "cleanliness" and "psychic fatigue," in
both men and women, are but a few of the many negative emotions
which can prevent fertility.

Wives whose sterility is psychogenic are usually highly narcissistic and they are often either hostile toward, or fearful of, their
mothers. The depth and dimension of their problem indicate the need
for psychotherapy, and the wise pastor will refer them to a psychiatrist rather than to plunge into waters that are too deep for him.

Some physicians regard negative emotions as contributing factors in 75 percent of infertile marriages. As culture becomes more
complex and as natural impulses are increasingly suppressed, psychogenic sterility will continue to increase. Of the one-third of the barren
unions without organic evidence to account for infertility, the principal cause is attributed to mental and emotional strain, chronic anxiety,
or unconscious fear which originates in early childhood and which
requires skillful psychotherapy as appropriate treatment.

Psychogenic sterility is effected through the endocrine and the
autonomic nervous systems as they upset hormonal balance and lead

to involuntary spasm, contraction and other irregular muscular functions. In each instance the psyche and soma have a reciprocal cause and effect relationship. Pseudocyesis and experiments in uterine physiology are two examples which clearly demonstrate the effect of emotions upon the reproductive system.

> Mrs. D, age 26, wanted a child the first year of marriage. After a year and a half of marriage, she came to church in maternity clothing and appeared to be about four months pregnant. She had "morning nausea" and other symptoms of pregnancy. At church she received "congratulations" joyfully. Two months later, she began to revert to her normal size. She saw her doctor. He attributed her condition to pseudocyesis and recommended psychiatric care. She did not consult a psychiatrist. She became deeply depressed. Her pastor tried to comfort her with generalities concerning trust in God. He read Psalm 23 and prayed that she be blessed in her time of grief. She was not comforted. She was hostile toward her husband who did not desire a baby at that time and who "would not cooperate." Her grief and depression became progressively worse until she had a "nervous breakdown." She was then taken to a psychiatrist and, under psychiatric care, she became "better." Her pastor felt unable to help her and, accordingly, did not discuss childlessness with her again.

As the pastor learns that the causes of sterility are psychogenic, or as he sees evidences of unconscious fear or of chronic anxiety, he should enlist the services of a psychiatrist. Apart from teamwork with a psychiatrist, his efforts will probably make "bad matters worse." Psychogenic sterility is relative and correctible through psychotherapy which reduces narcissistic motivations and which enables the person to accept his or her sex role. The pastor may, therefore, realistically support the hopes of those who receive psychiatric help for psychogenic sterility.

In direct contrast, a type of psychogenic sterility which is more frequently encountered than pseudocyesis is that which results in ovulation failure. Hysteria, obsessive-compulsive traits, acute feelings of guilt, self-inflicted punishment and neurotic depression are some of the many negative emotions which can bring about glandular disturbances and deficiencies and, in turn, prevent ovulation and menstruation. Following psychotherapy for emotional health and medical treatment for "general" health, these wives may begin to ovulate and prove to be highly fertile. That this is true is excellently and convincingly illustrated in a case study by Edith Jacobson of a wife, age 35, who, not having menstruated since she was 16, started ovulating following psychotherapy, became highly fertile, then neurotically regressed into rejection of further pregnancies and, once again, stopped ovulating and menstruating.[2]

Psychogenic sterility obviously requires psychiatric treatment. Pastoral counseling is concurrently indicated, however, to establish the person on a sound theological basis which promotes permanent success.

The psychogenic factors of idolatrous pride, narcissistic self-centeredness and rejection of sex roles are emotional causes of sterility, and are barriers of which the person is either unaware or unable to correct without help. As these persons achieve new insights and see themselves as they actually are, they are then in a position to be led by the pastor to make changes essential to repentance, reconciliation and a more abundant life.

Unknown.   After eliminating all known organic and psychic causes of infertility, some unknown or "X"-factor may account for failure to conceive. Pastoral counseling can help couples who have sought medical diagnosis and eliminated all known factors of infertility to commit their problem to God and to trust their parenthood destiny to divine care.

> Mr. C. kept his medical appointment, and his semen analysis revealed average fertility. The results of Mrs. C's tests revealed no organic cause of sterility. There were no gross emotional disturbances to indicate a psychogenic factor. The cause of their sterility remained unknown. Their pastor then led them to pray and to "leave it all in the hands of God." Four years later, they continued to hope for a baby, and did not wish to consider adoption. They acknowledged imperfection, but neither they nor their pastor attributed their barrenness to sin.

While couples should trust God, the pastor should neither state nor imply that human efforts are negated by the presence of the unknown, "X"-factor, or syndrome of "X"-factors. Surprising factors are continually being discovered and this should stimulate hope and

[2] "A Case of Sterility," The Psychoanalytic Quarterly, Fall, 1946, pp. 330–50.

continuing efforts. One such unknown factor that has been recently discovered by two physicians in the Netherlands, for instance, is a type of sperm-ovum "allergy" due to a "hostile" element in the blood. When these "antibodies" of the blood are eliminated, the prognosis for numerous couples who are now infertile will be very good. The experiments of Professor Albert Tyler of the California Institute of Technology confirm and supplement these findings.

Like Mr. and Mrs. C, many couples do not associate their infertility with sin. If a relationship exists between barrenness and sin, in many instances it is not known. In a few instances there is a definitely known, and traceable, relationship between sin and sterility, such as in sterility as caused by gonorrhea or by abuse of general health. In yet other instances, there appears to be no connection between sin and sterility. The basic consideration, however, is how to conform to God's creative laws of nature so that infertility can be overcome.

> Mr. and Mrs. F, ages 36 and 32, childless after twelve years of marriage, were devout, emotionally mature Christians. Neither had contracted venereal disease. Both sought maximum general health. No psychogenic factor was apparent to indicate the cause of sterility. Fertility tests showed both to be potential parents, yet they felt guilty. They told their pastor that they "must have sinned," that, otherwise, they would have had the desired children before now. They could not, however, think of any sin which they had committed that was "bad enough" to merit such "punishment." The pastor suggested that perhaps God was testing their faith rather than punishing them. He also reminded them of the universality of sin, and he "opened the door" to confession. Confession revealed that they had not committed "criminal" offenses. They had been faithful to each other. Their pre-marital sexual experiences were "above average." After confession, their pastor prayed with them. They then felt cleansed, and they felt that God would lift the "punishment" from them. One year later Mrs. F became pregnant, but she miscarried. Fifteen months thereafter she again conceived and, under expert medical care throughout the nine months of her pregnancy, gave birth to a healthy baby boy.

The experience of Mr. and Mrs. F is quite similar to that of Zechariah and Elizabeth in Luke 1:6–7, and as the pastor reads and interprets this passage of Scripture to them, they may, through the process of identification, be released from unfounded anxiety and feelings of guilt. While no person is perfect and all need the Saviour, infertility is probably not "punishment" in the majority of instances of childlessness. Zechariah and Elizabeth are but two of the many upstanding children of God mentioned in the Bible who are typical of a host of barren couples.

Since, however, the sense of guilt is strong in most infertile persons, the pastor may render a vital service by leading them to confess and to forsake rather than to cover and to ignore their sins (Romans 3:23, I John 1:8–10, and Proverbs 28:13). Before terminating the interview, however, the pastor can and should relieve the couple of needless anxiety by explaining to them the consistency and impartiality of the physiology of fertility which is true to the character of the Creator.

THE ROLE OF THE PASTOR IN PREVENTING STERILITY

More instances of sterility are preventable than inevitable, and pastoral care which leads to the prevention of these causal factors offers the most favorable prognosis for parenthood. Armed with knowledge of the cause of infertility, the pastor is now prepared to consider the preventive service which he can concurrently render to each of the oncoming generations.

In his teaching role, the pastor can help to prevent sterility. He can, for instance, organize a study group of young parents in the church who hope to become grandparents. He may entitle the discussion "Your Parental Responsibilities to Your Children's Children." In the first session he may teach them that, unless their children receive the proper physical and emotional nurture, and unless they are protected against sterilizing factors, they not only fail to meet their full parental responsibilities but also rob themselves of grandchildren. He can inform them that, at all ages, proper care of infectious diseases, sufficient food and hygenic care, early treatment of sexual and emotional disorders, wholesome physical and spiritual nurture, a balanced life which is not given to excesses and a sufficiency of vitamins such as A, B and E are essential to maximum general health and to fertility.

For boys especially, the pastor advised that constrictive clothing be avoided, and that parents expose their 5- to 10-year old sons to mumps rather than to risk permanent sterility from a possible later attack of this disease during early manhood. The pastor may lead them to see that "criminal" abortion destroys not only the baby but also the possibility of future pregnancies, and should not, therefore, be permitted. The pastor may use this opportunity to teach the parents how to nurture properly and to instruct positively their children on fertility and parenthood.

Concerning adolescent daughters, the pastor can recommend that parents take their teen-age daughters to a competent, non-frightening gynecologist for examination to detect and to correct early developing reproductive disorders, as well as to enhance ultimate "somatopsychic" sexuality, motherliness and motherhood.

To prevent psychogenic sterility of identification with the opposite sex, the pastor instructs parents in the importance of exemplary fulfillment of their sex role, and he cautions parents against statements which indicate rejection of their own basic sex role.

The pastor may inform the parents that complications from appendicitis, for instance, frequently nullify motherhood, and recommend that they take their young women of childbearing age to a doctor at the onset of the mildest attack of appendicitis.

The pastor should inform the parents of the ethical implications of concealing questionable fertility upon entering marriage, and should seek parental support of pre-marital fertility testing for those whose medical history creates doubts about their fertility. He may also suggest ways of strengthening the moral fiber of youth against illicit sexual relationships, especially since these relationships are the prevailing source of venereal diseases which are archenemies of fertility. To reserve their affections, as expressed in sexual intercourse, for marriage with a singleness of dedicated purpose is a worthy goal to uphold as guides for youth in temptation.

Since the degree and the type of interest in children significantly bear upon marital success, and since the idea of a child of "her own" is of enormous significance to the psychic life of "normal" women of every age, "the family" is a needful and normal addition to group discussions of "love, courtship and marriage." In instructing the youth of the church, the pastor may further the acceptance of basic sex roles, ethically support proper physical care and recommend pre-marital fertility tests to confirm fertility or to correct developing conditions which lead to sterility. By so doing, he not only ministers to prevent sterility but he also creates a favorable climate for later use of group resources by those who are infertile.

In his pulpit ministry, the pastor may discretely, timely and appropriately insert relevant facts and conclusions in some of his sermons to preserve and further fertility. These inserts, however, should not include the details of "why and wherefore." Sermons based upon such texts as Matthew 4:4, Romans 12:1–2 and Galatians 6:8, for instance, lend themselves readily to the additional ministry of preventing involuntary childlessness.

The teaching role of the pastor is not a "once and for all" task. The perennial need calls for purposive instruction. To meet the ethical, hygenic, nutritional and environmental needs of each generation, the educational program of the pastor in preventing sterility and in promoting parental fulfillment must be continuous.

Treatment and Prognosis.   Despite the best of preventive efforts, all causes and instances of infertility will not be eliminated, and the need for appropriate treatment will continue.

Having completed the diagnostic survey and learned the causes of infertility, approximately one-third of the couples are greeted with the "good news" that the recommended treatment is minor and the prognosis is "good." After two or three months of furthering general health and/or the removal of lesser obstructions by means of medications or minor surgery, these wives rejoice in pregnancy.

Mrs. T, for instance, as noted earlier, was treated for infection of the endometrium, and she became pregnant three months thereafter.

Mrs. B quit her job, took the prescribed vitamins, slept more and douched as directed prior to coitus to eliminate an excessive acidity, and conceived two months later.

Mrs. X had minor surgery. After the removal of cysts and treatment for infection, her gynecologist examined her and found that her tubes were open. Two months later she consulted her doctor as to why she was not pregnant, and he stated that they were "trying too hard" and too often, and were too excited. Instead of coitus every night, he informed her that a 48-hour interval was needful for full semen development. Two months later she missed her "period." She rushed to the doctor for a test to confirm pregnancy. He told her that at this early stage tests could not prove with certainty or reliability.

He instructed her to nourish her health as though she were pregnant for the sake of the baby's health and to lessen risks of miscarriage, and to come back in one month. The doctor's advice helped, but she was still very excited when she told her pastor, "I think I'm pregnant," and, after bringing him up-to-date on the medical developments, said, "It's so hard to wait! I try to be calm, but I just can't." The pastor erroneously advised, "Try not to think about it. When it comes to your mind, put it away by concentrating on something else." She responded, "I've tried that, but it doesn't work for me." Not knowing what to say, the pastor concluded the interview with the statement, "I'm going to pray for you. You pray, too, and try to be patient."

In counseling such couples as Mrs. X, the pastor helps by "hearing her out," by letting her talk until she "unwinds" completely. As they continue to talk, they usually are more relieved of tension, and they are also in a better position to achieve insights from associations and to come to their own conclusions.

Mrs. D shared the "good news" of possible pregnancy with her pastor, and told him of her excitement and impatience. He listened. After thirty minutes of uninterrupted talking, she came to these conclusions: "I feel better now. It helps to have someone like you to tell these things to. I'll make it! If I get too keyed up, I'll be back to see you." The pastor replied, "I'll be glad to see you anytime you desire to share with me what's on your heart." She then stated her religious conclusion: "I know that God cares, and He will not put more on us than we can bear. As a matter of fact, this waiting is so much better than before (during the diagnostic testing period) that I should be counting my blessings instead of "wishing away" a month of my life. I have faith in my doctor, and I have faith in God. It'll work out. I do want you to pray with me that my faith will be stronger." The pastor then led in such a prayer, and Mrs. D left in a much better frame of mind than when she came to her pastor for counseling.

Although a waiting period is involved, when the treatment is minor and the prognosis is good, most childless couples are hopeful and happy. They often proceed with zest, and the pastor's task is usually simplified to understanding listening and to supporting their own conclusions of the need for greater faith and for patient perseverance.

When the indicated treatment is major and prolonged in duration, and when the prognosis is doubtful or poor, the reaction of the couple is similar to, yet often more intense than, that which they experienced during their period of diagnostic testing. They tend to "give up" and to become depressed frequently and deeply. Even those who are best equipped to confront the complex infertility treatment manifest these tendencies.

> Mrs. M.D., age 28, whose husband was a physician, age 33, after three years of marriage and nine months of unsuccessful attempts to conceive, was taken to a gynecologist, who was a friend of the family, for diagnostic testing. The tests revealed that her tubes were blocked and that the only possible way to pregnancy was major surgery. The obstructed tube would have to be removed and another put in its place. Then, at this developmental point, the couple consulted their pastor, and the three of them came to the conclusion that, since the couple's desire for children of their own was intense, every means should be utilized, and that they should not abandon their efforts unless the prognosis became absolute and hopeless.
>
> Despite Mrs. M.D.'s intellectual and professional advantages, she had several dark moments of depression and fear, especially during her pre-surgery and convalescent period. She knew the risks, and she feared lest she be permanently damaged and a hysterectomy imperative. She stated to her pastor, "I often wonder if it's worth everything that's involved." As the pastor visited her in the hospital, she expressed her fears and feelings of depression. The pastor listened, and, finally, she returned to her original decision, that "no stone should be left unturned." Reassurance, relief and renewed efforts followed. Mrs. M.D. was closely observed and given the best of medical care; fourteen months after surgery she thrilled in her pregnancy to the first sure movements of the baby. She was very glad that she had not given up. She said to her pastor, "Thank you for not letting me quit trying." The pastor then informed her that she deserved the credit for those decisions, and that he was glad that he could, by lending a listening ear, help her to return to her true and basic desires.

The degree of the desire for children is the key to perseverance during complex medical treatment and doubtful prognosis, and the couple must return to their initial conclusion of continued efforts as long as there is a thread of hope, and reinforce their determination by rededication to the task, if they are to endure steadfastly and reassuredly to the end.

When sterility is absolute, the prognosis for children of their own is hopeless, and no medical treatment is indicated. Such couples experience intense and multi-dimensional grief, and the pastor's immediate task is ministering to the crisis of bereavement. All the emotions of those who have lost by death a close and beloved relative are usually encountered. The pastor's next task is to lead them to wholesome insights and right attitudes. Such couples have reached the stage where the sound consideration of the alternatives of artificial insemination, adoption or permanent childlessness is the road ahead.

FIVE

ATTITUDES
Of The STERILE COUPLE

In every phase of counseling the childless couple, attitudes are important. That the couple come to wholesome attitudes prior to the final interview is essential to successful counseling. A survey of Scriptural and contemporary attitudes toward infertility reveal negative attitudes which need to be eliminated and positive attitudes which should be cultivated.

The emotions of the barren may be either the cause or the result of infertility; thus the previously discussed psychogenic factor as a cause of sterility is both a background for, and an integral part of, the attitudes of many who are childless.

ATTITUDES TOWARD STERILITY
AS FOUND IN THE SCRIPTURES

The pastor who clearly perceives the attitudes toward barrenness as found in the Scriptures better understands the emotions of his contemporaries who are involuntarily childless and, in turn, more effectively uses the religious resources of the Scriptures in pastoral counseling. Instances which are similar to those of the Scriptures further identification, insight and reassurance. Contrasting instances help the couple to change in order that they may identify with the persons of the Bible who relate positively to God and who arrive at positive solutions to their problems. To enhance pastoral care, Scriptural attitudes toward infertility are interpreted from the perspective of the Hebrew wife, husband, rabbi and community, together with an interpretation of the purposes of God in fertility and sterility.

The perspective of Hebrew wives is reflected in the name "raham," or "womb," which indicates the value placed upon motherhood (Judges 5:30). In conception, the woman is viewed as contributing nothing of her essential self. Her function is regarded as a mere receptacle which molds shape and appearance of the child. Conception is mysteriously wrought by the power of God, and the male "seed" determines lineage, nature and character. When conception is impossible, the "deficiency" of childlessness is often indirectly, and partially, overcome through the "womb" of slaves who are regarded as property by which their mistress may possess the "seed" of her husband, and infertility is viewed as the principal basis for both polygamy and divorce.[1]

The supreme task of the Hebrew woman centers in family relatedness as wife and mother. From early childhood she is trained for this role, and failure to bear is, thus, for her, of paramount emotional significance. She is significant through her children; consequently, the barren wife feels disgraced and bereft of her chief blessing, and regards herself as insignificant as unfruitful chattel. Seldom, therefore, does she passively resign to sterility; instead, in cooperation with God, she usually uses every available resource to aid fertility. Prayer and mandrakes to relax the "womb" are two of the most frequently utilized resources. Charms, ablutions, incantations, pilgrimages and innumerable devices are sometimes used to enhance conception.

The most notable Scriptural instances of infertile women are Sarah, Rachel, Hannah and Elizabeth (Genesis 16, 17, 18, 21, 29, 30; I Samuel 1, 2; Luke 1, and Hebrews 11:11).

Sarah faced barrenness after menopause with honest skepticism. She unreasonably blamed Abraham for her infertility and, in jealous anger under intolerable emotional tension, she dealt harshly with fertile Hagar, who, in turn, despised her mistress. Sarah regarded infertility as a supreme calamity and fertility as a paramount blessing. In anxiety to conceive, and in the belief that intervention of Yahweh is essential to fertility, she fervently prayed. Her skepticism later turned to confident conviction and faithful trust in the promise and power of God to render her fertile.

Sarah said to Abraham, "Behold now, the Lord has prevented me from bearing children; go into my maid; it may be that I shall obtain children by her" (Genesis 16:2). Sarah was, in effect, saying to Abraham, "God is punishing me. I am not all that I should be as a

---

[1] *See* David R. Mace, *Hebrew Marriage* (London: The Epworth Press, 1953), pp. 201–15.

woman, and I have no right to hold you and to deny you of children. I release you. You have my permission to sleep with Hagar."

Although Sarah gave her permission in conformity to the social order, jealousy shows that she did not actually desire such a "triangle." Hagar, "the other woman," "conceived; and when she saw that she had conceived, she looked with contempt on her mistress." And Sarah said to Abraham, "May the wrong done to me be on you! I gave my maid to your embrace, and when she saw that she had conceived, she looked on me with contempt. May the Lord judge between you and me!" Abraham said to Sarah, "Behold, your maid is in your power; do to her as you please." Then Sarah "dealt harshly with her" (Genesis 16: 4–6). As Sarah lay alone upon her bed and thought of her husband who was, at that time, embracing another woman, deep hurt, jealousy and resentment were normal emotional reactions. Hagar, though socially inferior, felt superior to her mistress as a woman after conception, and she "lorded it over" Sarah. Sarah retaliated and said, in effect, to Abraham, "The way things now stand is intolerable. It's either Hagar or me. It's up to you to decide, but one of us has to go." Although the law supported such a "triangle," polygamy or divorce has never proved to be a satisfactory solution to childlessness.

Rachel, the favored wife of Jacob, was barren. The Lord saw that Leah was "hated," and opened her "womb," and, thereby, protected the less favored wife. Rachel then envied Leah and said to Jacob, "Give me children or I shall die" (Genesis 30:1). Sorrow, shame, reproach, humiliation, accusation of husband and a sense of ultimate calamity are reflected in the attitudes of Rachel.

Although Rachel was reared to believe that barrenness was exclusively the "fault" of the wife, she "blamed" Jacob. She may not have been reasoning, but, conceivably, she was feeling, "Jacob, if you gave more time and attention to me, I would get pregnant. I don't want to live if I can't have a baby. You can and you must cause me to conceive." Hence, the tendency to shift the responsibility for infertility to one's mate is not new.

In self-reproach, Hannah's heart smote her for being barren. She was tense from social pressure, from persecution by Peniah, and from unfulfilled desire to bear a child of Elkanah, her husband. Her wounds of grief for failure to give him a child were opened afresh by his apparently well-intended, yet misdirected, efforts to reassure and comfort her. Her behavior of fasting and bitter weeping indicates the depth of her distress.

The pressure of the presence of fertile Peniah became so great that Hannah lost her appetite and wept bitterly. Elkanah, approaching her emotional problems on an intellectual basis, said, "Hannah, why do you weep? And why do you not eat? And why is your heart sad? Am I not more to you than ten sons?" (1 Samuel 1:8). This made bad matters worse. One person cannot replace another and, while a person may be grateful for his blessings, he rightfully mourns his losses. The comparative approach, whereby an infertile person is informed that things are better for them in some ways than they are for others, has always failed to bring the desired comfort and reassurance.

Hannah prayed long and fervently. Her depth of emotional anguish, as manifest by lips which moved but produced no sound, led Elkanah to rebuke her for drunkenness. Hannah, sensibly replying that he was mistaken, said, "I am a woman sorely troubled; I have drunk neither wine nor strong drink, but I have been pouring out my soul before the Lord. Do not regard your maid-servant as a base woman, for all along I have been speaking out of my great anxiety and vexation." (1 Samuel 1:15–16). Hannah did not regard herself as an evil person who deserved reproach and punishment, and, although she felt reproach, she persevered in her quest for both the favor of God and of her husband. She had been treated like a scorned dog, but she remained friendly and entreating; then she gained the favor of her husband and of God, and she shared her son with God in dedicated service.

Elizabeth and her husband were "righteous" and "blameless," yet she felt reproach so keenly that she confined herself to her home and did not reappear in public until she was five months pregnant and obviously no longer subject to the social stigma of sterility (Luke 1:24–25). The lack of community acceptance and the feeling of not belonging caused Elizabeth and most of the childless Hebrew wives to withdraw into seclusion and to seldom appear in public. They suffered silently, intensely and alone, and as tersely noted in the Wisdom literature, the "womb" that is restrained from bearing is insatiably impoverished (Proverbs 30:16).

The attitudes of the barren wives of the Scripture differ primarily in degree rather than in kind, with the exception of Rebekah, who apparently left the responsibility of fertility completely to Isaac, who, in intercessory prayer, effectively entreated the Lord (Genesis 25:21). Although these wives felt reproach and were led to assume that they were guilty and, consequently, deserved punishment, there is no indication that these women knew of specific sins which caused sterility. Most of them walked in integrity and moral uprightness, and they viewed their character with confidence.

Most Hebrew wives erroneously confused or equated the sovereignty of God with the decisive cause of all sterility. This is theologically dangerous in that human accountability is minimized and the nature of God is distortedly portrayed to appear partial and unjust. God's sovereignty in fertility and sterility, however, is operative through His creative physiological laws, and whosoever fails to meet or to comply with these laws is inevitably infertile.

In each of the Scriptural instances cited, the infertile wife ultimately conceives and sings joyful praises to God. As poetically expressed in the Psalms, "He maketh the barren woman a home, making her the joyous mother of children. Praise the Lord!" (Psalm 113:9). Although the pastor can point to no permanently barren couple of the Scriptures with whom the hopelessly sterile persons of today may identify, the Scriptures do speak constructively to their emotions. Deuteronomy 33:27, Joshua 1:9, Psalm 16:8, Psalm 27:1–10, Psalm 46, Isaiah 40:28–31, Isaiah 41:13, Matthew 5:4, Matthew 11:28, John 16:33, Romans 8:38–39, Romans 14:7–8 and 2 Corinthians 4:13–18 are cited to illustrate the powerful resources of the Scriptures for the emotional needs of the permanently sterile couple.

The perspective of the Hebrew husband is quite different from that of his wife. He regards himself as fertile and not responsible for her barrenness. In each of the noted instances of the Old Testament, the husband's fertility appears to be fully substantiated by his becoming a father in polygamous union. In actuality, however, the possibility of selective sterility is not scientifically precluded. Abraham could have had a "low" fertility, for instance, and been able to impregnate a highly fertile Hagar, but not have been able to have children by a woman of "low" fertility, which was possibly the case with Sarah.

Although the recognized possibility of male sterility is apparently limited to voluntary or involuntary emasculation, lack of recognition does not necessarily negate the existence of other male factors in sterile matings. Selective sterility may be evidenced in the marriages of the patriarchs in which there is infertility with the wife but fertility with the handmaidens, which may scientifically indicate a low fertility index of either or both husband and wife.

The Hebrew law which provides for progeny to perpetuate the lineage of deceased childless husbands (Genesis 38; Deuteronomy 25:5, and Matthew 22:24–28) may not be associated in the Hebrew mind with infertility, but it logically suggests the possibility of the male factor as a cause of infertility when neither wife nor concubine conceive after years of repeated efforts.

The Israelites confronted sexual "uncleanness" and sought the prevention of the moral and physical ruin which it often brought. They interpreted fertility not only of men and women but also of plants and animals as a blessing from God which is conditioned upon fidelity to Him within the covenant relationship (Deuteronomy 7:12–16); thus they strongly opposed adultery, and the writers of Proverbs (chapter 7) and of 1 Corinthians (6:18) warn of the killing effect of illicit coitus upon the body and spirit of the male. The diseases could have been gonorrhea or syphilis which can result in male as well as in female sterility.

From a scientific approach, it is thus conceivable that the Scripture implies far more concerning male sterility than the ancient Hebrews envisioned, admitted, accepted or supported.

Perceiving himself to be beyond "blame" for his wife's barrenness, the significant emotions of the Hebrew husband are his attitudes toward his infertile wife. These attitudes are discernible from his marital behavior. Abraham, for instance, dealt kindly and justly with Sarah, and though he, too, was old, he was not skeptical of begetting a son by her. Although Isaac's fertility was not questioned, he prayed to God that Rebekah's sterility be overcome, and thus relieved her of the burden of responsibility for her barrenness. Jacob resented the implications of Rachel that he was withholding conception from her, and he angrily asked her if she thought that he were God. Elkanah loved Hannah and responded to her with exceptional kindness and reassuring efforts, until he thought that she had taken her tragedy to the extremity of drunkenness. Zechariah seemed to be positively related to Elizabeth but he, more strongly than Sarah, skeptically questioned God (Genesis 16, 17, 18, 21, 29, 30; 1 Samuel 1, 2, and Luke 1).

The pastor of fertile husbands whose wives are infertile may lead the husbands to identify with such men as Abraham, Isaac and Elkanah, and thereby lead them to constructive attitudes. The pastor cannot draw a parallel situation between the infertile husbands of today and the fertile husbands of the Scripture, and is not, therefore, to uphold their attitudes which reject, as do the husbands of the Scriptures, the possibility of their sterility. The pastor can, however, interpret such passages of Scripture as Matthew 19:12 to help the infertile husband of today to see that he is not alone in the problem and to show him that his sterility does not place him beyond the purposes of God.

The Hebrew husband envisions immortality or reincarnation through his sons. He feels that, if not by his wife, then by another he must father sons. To beget sons looms so large in his life that the emasculated male is excommunicated except for mitigating circumstances of forced sterilization (Deuteronomy 23:1 and Isaiah 56:31–35). Current concepts of immortality through children are not as strong, and the pastor may reassure infertile husbands that their sterility will not meet with rejection or excommunication by God, himself, or the church. The pastor may state that immortality, rather than being limited to procreation, may be achieved by such means as a memorable Christian life. He may inform the sterile husband that a son may scandalize the memory of a godly father (1 Samuel 3:13), and, conversely, that a childless man may be a spiritual father to many people who aspire to be like him.

The perspective of the Hebrew rabbi is equated with that of the Hebrew community. The failure to bear children is regarded as an indication of divine displeasure which God manifests through the withdrawal of blessings and the punishment of a "closed" or "miscarrying womb." So important is early marital adjustment and parenthood to the community concept of human destiny that the Israelite nation exempts the husband from military service for at least one year after marriage. "When a man is newly married, he shall not go out with the army or be charged with any business; he shall be free at home one year, to be happy with his wife whom he has taken" (Deuteronomy 24:5). The best way that he can make his wife happy is to cause her to conceive during the initial year of marriage. That is his business, and he is not to be overworked or detracted from this, the principal means of adjustment within marriage. From generation to generation, a continuation of the male line which preserved the family is the supreme consideration and, despite such pressing demands as the maintenance of military and economic security, all pursuits are subordinate to fertility and propagation.

The Hebrew couple must have children before ten years of marriage; otherwise, the Jewish talmud makes divorce mandatory, and the barren wife is regarded with the poor, the blind and the leprous as dead. With the initial year in which the couple has no responsibility except fertility, and with nine additional years of "grace," this ruling was accepted as generously just. They felt that if a wife did not conceive in ten years, then she never would. Post-exilic Jewish law requires a minimum of one son and one daughter, forbids castration of man, fowl and beast, and supports divorce of infertile unions to prevent "waste of nature." To the Hebrew rabbi, sterility is, therefore, a major issue. He urges paternity, condemns childless wives, excommunicates emasculated men and supports divorce on the basis of barrenness.[2]

To view sterility as a curse from God, however, is contradictory to the experience of Zechariah and Elizabeth, barren persons who were "righteous" before God and "blameless" (Luke 1:5-7). By means of such Scriptural examples, the pastor may relieve many upstanding couples of needless fear, deep depression and doubt.

Neither the contemporary community nor the modern minister regard a physical continuation of the male lineage as either mandatory or of paramount significance, and divorce is neither indicated nor approved on the basis of infertility.

The interpreted purposes of God in fertility and sterility necessitate an understanding of His purposes of marriage. He wills that couples become "one flesh," and this is the basic and essential purpose of marriage. He purposes that children be born of married couples rather than of illicit unions, but that couples "multiply and fill the earth" is a promised blessing rather than a command of God or a requirement of marriage which may prove impossible to keep. Children are a "heritage from the Lord," and fertility, which is symbolized by a "land flowing with milk and honey," is a prominent Old Testament hallmark of divine pleasure, but the Scriptures neither state nor imply that God purposes a temporary union which must either be

[2] *See* Louis M. Epstein, *Sex Laws and Customs in Judaism* (New York: Block Publishing Company, 1948), pp. 138-45.

fruitful or be dissolved. Scriptural instances of sterility are temporary and serve as a wholesome means of disciplining disciples, of strengthening faith and patience and of preparing the couple for exceptional parenthood (Genesis 1:27–28; 2:24; Psalm 127:3–4; Exodus 3:8).

CONTEMPORARY ATTITUDES TOWARD STERILITY

The multiple emotions of the sterile may be both causal and symptomatic in nature, the results of innumerable influences. In addition to the current interpretations of the purposes of God in fertility and sterility which are mentioned above, the pastor who would evaluate properly the attitudes of the childless couple thus needs to understand the emotional reactions of the wife, husband, ministers of various faiths and community.

In past and contemporary experience, couples who are involuntarily childless suffer severely. Accepting and working through their infertility problem is usually an intensely painful emotional experience. When the desire for children is strong, regardless of the cause of barrenness, infertility creates a domestic situation which is heavy for the best of marriages and which is intolerable for those whose marital relationships are weak. One of the most painful emotional experiences that can come to a person is experienced when he becomes aware of his sterility. The tragedy of involuntary childlessness is a two-edged sword which cuts "going and coming." As their thoughts go to the desired yet denied children, they are tragically cut in grief, and as their thoughts come back to self, the ego is cut to feelings of inadequacy, inferiority and insecurity.

In contemporary experience, as previously illustrated in the case of Mrs. T, paralyzing shock and intense anxiety are frequently the initial reactions to the discovery of sterility. For many women, and particularly for those who regard reproduction as the prime reason for marriage, sterility is the root-cause of their deepest despondency. The sterile wife feels the torture of frustrated "natural" longings, and she feels guilty of depriving her husband. These emotional reactions arise from a biologically "instinctive" and culturally learned foundation. Most infertile wives also feel physically inferior and, left to themselves, they sometimes develop a distinctly neurotic personality structure.

In reaction to the sterility trauma, some women transfer the trauma to existing organic disturbances, while others deny emotional shock, envy mothers and pregnant women, dominate grief by masculine self-assertion, obsessively seek pregnancy or resign to infertility and mother their husbands. These attitudes and reactions show the urgency of the crisis and the need for immediate pastoral care.

The pastor comforts the sterile wife in her crisis of bereavement, and seeks to lead her to face reality, to mourn, to work through her feelings of guilt, inferiority, and hostility, and to confess and receive forgiveness as indicated. The pastor uses the Bible effectively as he helps her to see the many similiarities between her reactions and those of the barren women of the Scriptures.

To minister adequately to the needs of the childless couple, the pastor neither judges nor is alarmed by anything that is revealed to him. His counseling ministry is helped by assuring the sterile wife that he will not betray her confidence. The pastor's faith in God, in life and in her should be verbally affirmed and experientially verified, and, in a permissive rather than in a dogmatic authoritarian atmosphere, the need for pastor instruction in significant Christian doctrine and ethic can and should be met. The pastor helps by assuring her of the ultimate purposes of God which triumph over evil and death, and by reaffirming the power and sufficiency of God to meet every need. In such a relationship, she usually experiences understanding, new insights, creative growth, emotional support and release from tension and contradictory feelings. Her adjustment is complete when, in pastoral counseling, she dies to self and comes alive to others in the living dimension of faith, fellowship and service. Pastoral counseling for an hour, once or twice a week, over a period of ten or more weeks, may be needful to accomplish these positive results.

When the wife is childless due to her husband's infertility, the pastor ministers to a complex marital problem. The wife is usually more disturbed when her husband is "irretrievably" sterile than when she is the cause of barrenness, and her feelings for her husband undergo a marked, negative change. In varying degrees, she inevitably bears resentment and thinks less of him as a man. If she bites with a bitter tongue, then the husband will have to be strong in character to maintain the marriage. She can so magnify her devaluation of him that she will no longer be able to tolerate their marriage. Three types of women in reaction to male sterility are the masculine-aggressive, the cooperatively ambitious and the motherly. The reactions and subsequent adjustments of barren wives are conditioned by the causes of sterility, the degree of genuine motherliness and the husband-wife relationship. Such conditioning factors as these are highly important, and should, therefore, be kept in mind by the pastor who counsels childless couples.

Unresolved problems relating to sex seem to come to the forefront at menopause in a perspective which is grossly magnified out of due proportion. The sterile wife may find menopause accompanied by disease and deep despair, and her psychological reaction may be that of "sour grapes," impatience, and intolerance toward children. A team approach of pastor, physician, and psychiatrist is most desirable, if not absolutely essential, to meet her emotional needs.

The complexity and emotional depth of the sterile couple's marital conflict may indicate referral. Intense, unconscious, negative emotions of some masculine-aggressive women, for instance, indicate the need for referral to a psychiatrist. The pastor may also have neither the aptitude nor the specialized training that is needful for intense marriage and family counseling, and may, therefore, feel the need for referral to a fellow minister who meets these qualifications. The complexity of the problem may necessitate several months of counseling, and, regardless of his qualifications, fortunate indeed is the busy pastor whose time is exceedingly limited when he can refer such persons to a reputable and readily accessible marriage and family counseling center.

The emotional reaction of the husband to involuntary childlessness is strongly conditioned by culture. To be respected and self-respecting in America, men usually feel that they must have a "job," a car, a wife and children; otherwise, they often feel unsatisfied, dishonored and rejected. Common in male sterility are feelings of guilt, inefficiency, self-pity, frustration for depriving his wife, a strong sense of inferiority and personal devaluation. He tends to reject the reality of sterility and to hide his feelings of failure.

Mr. K, age 26, had been injured while playing football in high school. His left testicle atrophied. His right was normal. His semen analysis was 30 percent. He felt inferior, rejected and guilty of denying his wife. He tried to ignore reality. He overcompensated academically in his scholastic quest to excel all others. Constructive criticism of his work was interpreted as a personal insult. He tried hard to impregnate his wife, but he failed to do so. In a permissive relationship with his pastor, he found acceptance. He then began to face reality and, increasingly, to express his feelings.

Although the husband mourns his fertility loss, his bereavement usually finds means of expression which differ from those of his wife. His sense of loneliness, guilt and rejection are acute. The pastor ministers to his needs by leading him to an acceptance with God, himself and the church. He offers hope to the sterile husband in the vision of opportunities for achievement which does not necessitate procreation, and seeks to lead him to a realistic appraisal, and acceptance of, his limitations, and to a commitment which constructively utilizes his potential. The pastor may help by leading infertile husbands to resolve with the Apostle Paul: "Forgetting what lies behind and straining forward to what lies ahead, I press on toward the goal for the prize of the upward call of God in Christ Jesus" (Philippians 3:13–14).

Infertile husbands often desire confirmation of virility through fertility. The husband who continues to doubt his virility after being informed that virility is actually confirmed by coitus rather than by fertility probably has unconscious associations with castration anxieties. His behavior may also reflect unconscious feelings toward his mother.

When the husband is childless due to an infertile wife, he often feels threatened, and he sometimes becomes bitter to the point of divorce. The pastor has ample Scriptural examples of infertile wives and fertile husbands, and, by using these examples, he may lead the husband from bitter thoughts of divorce to cooperative, prayerful concern for his wife. Abraham, Isaac, Elkanah and Zechariah are especially commendable in their reactions to their barren wives (Genesis 16, 17, 18, 21, 29, 30; 1 Samuel 1, and Luke 1).

The majority of modern Protestant pastors show little or no concern for the problem of involuntary childlessness. A surprisingly large number of today's pastors have given very little thought to the childless couples in their community. A large number of pastors have no definite opinion or conviction on the subject. The problem has been left so completely alone that it has not been a part of the pastor's traditional training and ministry. He is already "swamped" with work, and is not eager to take on more, particularly when it is as complex in nature and prolonged in duration as the infertility problem. In most instances, contemporary Protestant pastors who make conscientious efforts toward resolving the infertility problems of the childless are those who have personally experienced the pain of sterility or who have close relatives and friends in need of his counsel.

The modern Protestant pastor who counsels the childless couple does not regard sterility as a paramount issue. He usually takes a more individualistic approach. He neither urges nor disapproves parenthood. He does not censure, condemn, or reject. He neither excommunicates for sterilization nor supports divorce for childlessness. The hopelessly sterile couple will generally find the modern pastor approachable, understanding and helpful in sharing the heavy burden of barrenness.

The position of the Roman Catholic priests of today is somewhere between that of the ancient rabbi and that of today's Protestant minister. He forbids contraceptives and exerts pressure upon couples to have large families, but he does not excommunicate or support divorce for involuntary childlessness. He ministers to their needs more effectively than the ancient rabbi, but fails to follow through with counseling.

The ancient rabbi and the contemporary rabbi have the same Book of Law, but, contemporarily, while the rabbi encourages couples to have children, punitive measures are either completely eliminated or considerably tempered. The degree of liberality varies with the extent of his "orthodox" or "reform" convictions.

The usual reaction of modern communities to infertile marriages is to commend fertility and to criticize infertility as irresponsible. The American cultural pattern generally expects the couple to bear at least one child.

The social pressure of the community upon childless couples is brought to bear by many persons in numerous ways. Unresolved sibling rivalry, for instance, can create a great deal of tension for the infertile.

As they were "growing-up," Esau-like B teased his Jacob-like brother J for not having hair on his chest. Both married. B was infertile and childless after seven years of marriage. J became a father after two years of marriage and said to B, "It takes more than hair on your chest to make a man." Then J made B "fighting mad" when he added tauntingly, "I could help you out, but I don't think you'd appreciate it." And beautiful and haughty, yet sterile, Rachel-like B was the "belle of the ball," but her older, wallflower, Leah-like sister M was highly fertile. After the birth of her third child, M said to B, "You were more popular than I when we were 'growing up,' and you married before I did, but I caught up with you and now I'm way ahead of you. I guess it's true, 'Beauty is skin deep' and 'It's what's inside you that counts.' "

Many parents continue to bring pressure upon their married, yet childless, children by telling them what they "ought to do."

A mother, and would-be grandmother, for instance, said to her daughter, R, "I know it's no picnic having a baby, but you ought to have at least one, and you ought not to put it off any longer. You wait until your hips get "set" and you'll have a hard time, sure enough. You ought to have a baby, and the sooner the better." In a pleading tone of self-pity the mother added, "I hope you start your family before your Daddy and I get so old that we can't enjoy our grandchildren."

Under the guise of "humor," many friends exert cruel pressure upon the childless couple. Some who feel that their childless friends are taking themselves too seriously try to "joke them out of it," while others use "humor" to disguise their barbs and bragging. A few of the many so-called "jokes" include the following statements:

"Boy, what you need is a lot of oysters and steaks."

"Isn't your wife feeding you right? Come over to my house and try of our cooking. If that don't put 'lead in your pencil,' I don't know what will."

"That water you're drinking must not be any good. Want me to send over a barrel of our water?"

"My husband just has to hang his pants on the foot of our bed and I get pregnant. Maybe our husbands ought to get together for a little talk. Ha Ha."

A 28-year-old father of four said to a 30-year-old infertile friend of a 32-year-old neighbor who had recently become a father for the first time, "Well, the old boy's not dead yet, after all."

A fertile father of six said to his infertile friend and classmate when leaving from a picnic, "Bring the kids . . . and come to see us."

"You can't tell a book by its cover."

"I'll tell you your trouble. You're just not holding your mouth right."

Another means of community pressure is exerted through "sins of omission," and what is not done often hurts more than what is done. Couples with children often leave childless couples off their "invitation list" when planning "socials." They rationalize their rejection by saying that everyone will be talking about their children, and that could be embarrassing to them.

The prevailing community attitude continues to cultivate in the sterile couple a sense of guilt, inferiority and inadequacy. Community pressures thus continue to deal unjustly with those who diligently, yet unsuccessfully, seek fertility. Although they are not physically cast beyond the "city limits," the emotional impact is quite similar. To be rejected for infertility as a "fifth wheel" and to be as "lost in a crowd" as a "country boy" in a strange, big city may, in actuality, be far worse from the perspective of the childless couple than the "clean-cut" excommunication of the ancient Hebrew community.

The modern community does not support divorce for sterility, yet group pressure helps to create an atmosphere which divides childless couples. To be criticized and to be "made fun of" by those whose opinions they value and whose approval they seek may be a far stronger "pull" than the bonds of matrimony, a crosscurrent that is too strong for the weak to withstand. Since "none of us lives to himself, and none of us dies to himself" (Romans 14:7), citizens of America's communities need to become more alertly aware of corporate responsibility, sin and guilt as the "keeper" of their childless couples.

In his preaching and teaching role, the understanding and compassionate pastor leads the church away from thoughtless jests which cruelly hurt. He leads persons to depart from a judgmental spirit lest they who also are limited and sinful be condemned. He molds a spirit of concern which is similar to his own, and by his empathy for childless couples whom he is assisting, the godly pastor transmits through example a positive reconstruction of community attitudes. By example and precept, he leads the Christian community to attitudes which accept the couple under God as "brothers" who are their equal in Christ.

SIX

ARTIFICIAL INSEMINATION

When couples are childless due to the male factor, an exploration of the alternatives of artificial insemination is indicated. A sense of satisfaction follows a thorough coverage of all the alternatives, and even when couples do not desire artificial insemination, it is better for them to come to a definite and clear decision in the light of all the facts than for them to ponder the advisability of this alternative later and, consequently, to become anxious with fearful doubts. The time to consider artificial insemination, for instance, is before rather than after adoption.

Artificial insemination is the introduction of semen of the husband or of a donor into the genital tract of the female without sexual intercourse. In infertile unions the sperm of the husband is preferable but often inadequate; hence, this medical procedure is usually associated with donor semen. A third possibility in artificial insemination is the introduction of semen of both the husband and of a donor in combination.

When the semen of the husband is qualitatively "good" but quantitatively "low," the doctor may suggest that the couple try a "fertilo-pak." Following coitus, a "fertilo-pak" may be inserted much the same as a "diaphragm" to contain all the semen at the "mouth" of the uterus, the location most favorable for conception; then, if that fails, artificial insemination by means of the husband's semen only may be advised.

The use of the husband's semen only seldom presents serious ethical problems, and for husbands whose sperm is of good quality, though low in quantity, the percentage of success by this method is high. A few persons, however, may object to the means of collecting the semen or to any aid on the grounds that it is contrary to "nature." The use of the husband's semen only is by far the most satisfactory and advisable means of artificial insemination, and may thus be supported unreservedly. Unfortunately, however, the husband's semen is not adequate in the majority of instances in which artificial insemination is indicated; hence, this alternative is primarily, though not exclusively, associated with donor semen.

The use of the husband's semen in combination with a donor's semen is a possibility. In such instances, the husband may choose to believe that it was his semen that actually impregnated his wife and that the donor's semen served as a "booster" only which launched his semen to the desired destination. When the physical characteristics of the donor and of the husband are closely "matched," then the similarities of the baby to the husband may cause him to rationalize that the child has to be his because it "looks just like him." In varying degrees, the wife may also concur with these desired thoughts. This alternative is conducive to wishful thinking, self-deception, and anxious doubts, and is therefore opposed because of its potential and probability for creating more problems than it could possibly resolve.

The donor factor is the crux of the problem in the alternative of artificial insemination and is, therefore, given comprehensive coverage as viewed by those favoring as well as those opposing its practice. Major aspects are explored, "pro and con," from the perspective of the several persons concerned.

IN FAVOR OF ARTIFICIAL INSEMINATION

Those favoring artificial insemination by donor semen seek its justification in the ethics of expediency. They reason that couples of "mixed marriages" cannot adopt; that not enough babies are available for adoption; that this method of impregnation is eugenically sound, and that for many it makes marriage happier and more complete.

Some authorities regard artificial insemination as "therapeutic," moral and commendable rather than "artificial," adulterous and unnatural. They view this alternative as superior to adoption because the baby inherits physical qualities of the mother now given the opportunity to bear her own child and fulfill her motherly urge, and, by surrounding the medical procedure of donor insemination with absolute secrecy, the stigma of sterility is removed from both the husband and the wife.

The opinions of the husband, wife and donor who favor artificial insemination usually concur with the ethical concepts of one sterile husband who said:

> "If another man slept with my wife, there would be plenty wrong with it, but, as it is, I see nothing wrong with it. There's nothing personal about it. I can't see much difference between that and my wife having a blood transfusion from some man she doesn't know. Both are for the sake of a life . . . one to save a life, and the other to add a life. We're not narrow-minded, and if my wife wants a baby that way, then I have no objections."

While recognizing legal problems, those who favor artificial insemination do not regard them as insurmountable. If the donor does not know the recipient of his semen, then the threat of blackmail is eliminated, and, if the donor is paid for his semen, then a binding contract can be drawn which, in similarity to other sales, relinquishes all claims which he may have to the "property," and the couple need not fear that the child will be taken away from them. With the assistance of a thoroughly competent lawyer, the legal aspects need not prevent fertility by this "therapeutic" means.

Those who cast their vote for donor insemination now, however, do so restrictedly. They believe that the many psychological, social, moral and legal implications limit the field of qualified candidates to the intellectually and emotionally mature only. For all others, donor insemination would be completely out of the question.

Even though artificial insemination is often an expensive and inconvenient procedure, those favoring this "therapy" reason that "it is worth it," and many women who desperately want a baby of their own have said that they would give "anything" to beget children.

The history of this means of impregnation begins in Italy in 1793 and is currently the method of effecting thousands of pregnancies. The number in America of those who favor and seek fertility by this means is increasing and, as the facts become more generally known, the number will probably become even greater. Regardless of personal convictions, this procedure is likely to increase to the extent that most pastors will no longer be able to completely ignore it.

A better understanding of the psychological aspects of those who are most intimately involved and who favor artificial insemination, namely, the donor, the wife and the husband, may enable the pastor to counsel with greater understanding. The donor is a key person in this triune consideration, and he has feelings which need to be understood.

A healthy, active, medical intern, Mr. I, age 27, of good heritage, the father of two sturdy sons, studied the needs of the sterile and decided to become a donor. He confided to his pastor: "Some may wonder why a person would even consider becoming a donor, but, actually, there are many good reasons. This is another and new way that I can prevent needless suffering for those wives who are 'eating their heart out' in their desire to have a baby. I view the procedure as very humanitarian, and, at the same time that I'm helping them, I'm also helping myself and, as you know, an intern could well use the extra money. No one is harmed. Everyone is helped." He continued quite honestly, "That's not the entire picture, though. To be quite frank with you, it bolsters my ego to make this specialized contribution to my fellow man, and it would make me feel good to become the father of at least a hundred children." The pastor paused, but Mr. I did not continue; then the pastor said: "How does your wife feel about it?" "She doesn't know," replied Mr. I. "I haven't told her, and I don't intend to tell her. She might not understand, and she might let her imagination make a problem of it. Actually, she doesn't need to know. It's another aspect of my 'work,' as I see it, and there are many medical technicalities which have no place in the 'family circle,' and are not mentioned. It would likely result in confusion rather than in clarification. The pastor nodded his head and reflected: "You seem to have given this thorough thought. You have no doubts, no reservations about being a donor?" "None whatsoever," replied Mr. I. The pastor did not argue the ethics of the decisions. "I understand, and I am glad to know that you acted in good faith. Thank you for sharing these thoughts with me," said the pastor in concluding the informal "interview."

The ego of the donor is a factor which merits further study. The donor may be deluded with grandeur or he may be over-compensating for felt weaknesses, and, consequently, he may also need counseling. Monetary remuneration is not likely to be the principal reason for his "donation," and the stated or conscious reasons may not reveal the prime movers which motivate his investment in the sperm "bank."

The husband is the one who is "left out" by donor insemination. He is forced to acknowledge his physical limitations. That he consents to "help" from a fertile man is important. The baby will not be his own "flesh and blood." He remains childless, thus his emotional response to artificial insemination by donor semen is probably the most significant of all who are directly involved.

Mr. S, age 32, married for ten years, became sterile one year after marriage as a result of an automobile accident. His wife, age 30, had yearned for a baby ever since the results of the accident were known. Mr. S was tormented that he could not "give her a baby," and he offered to "set her free" so that she could marry again. She avowed her love for him as stronger than her longing to conceive, and she gave no consideration to the offered alternative. She did not desire to adopt, and the only alternative that she would consider was artificial insemination. When the pastor visited their home after the mother and daughter returned from the hospital, Mr. S told him how he felt. "I love my wife dearly," said Mr. S, "and I just couldn't stand to see her suffer any longer. I felt that I could stand most anything better than that. My wife is happy now. She seems happier than she has been for years. I've suffered more than anyone will ever know because of that accident and what it did to me, but I feel better now because she feels better. It took me quite a while to make up my mind to see this through, but I'm glad that I did . . . for her sake." The pastor read Psalm 127, and led in a prayer of thanksgiving for the couple and for the baby, and he asked God's blessings to preserve and to enhance the strong bonds of love which now exist in the home.

The husband rightly mourns his loss of fertility, and he needs to come to terms with his physical limitations. As in the case of Mr. S, strong love can surmount countless obstacles and make other burdens bearable. To further a love that is stronger than death to fatherhood is one means of pastoral support in such instances of counseling.

The childless wife who intensely desires to have a baby benefits most by artificial insemination. This procedure may make her "fondest dreams" of fertility come true. She thus has more reasons for desiring this alternative than anyone else, and to help her to realize her parental ambitions is the principal purpose of this "therapy." While the circumstances of Mrs. S, as illustrated above, are seldom encountered, her desire for children is typical of those childless wives who favor artificial insemination in preference to other alternatives. Another typical situation follows.

Mrs. A, age 30, married eight years, and her husband, age 34, sought fertility testing after seven years of unsuccessful efforts to conceive. Mr. A's sterility was almost absolute, and artificial insemination by donor semen was suggested by the doctor for their consideration. Mrs. A secured all available information, weighed each aspect carefully over a period of six months, then sought her pastor's confirmation of her decision. She explained: "Ever since I was a little girl playing with dolls, I've wanted a baby of my own. I grew up with those thoughts, and they are a part of me. I wouldn't divorce my husband and I wouldn't be unfaithful to him, even though a part of me would die if I couldn't have children, but I don't think I'm sinning by doing this . . . and . . . it's a relief to me to know that something may yet be done. What do you think? Is it wrong for me to go ahead as planned?" The pastor replied with a question: "Have you considered how this might affect your husband and your feelings toward him?" She nodded "yes." "Can you accept him and the baby without a breach on your part in your relationships?" She again nodded in the affirmative. "The way I see it," continued the pastor, "you're not actually committing adultery, and if you are fully satisfied that this is the best for all concerned, then 'blessings upon you.' "

Devoutly religious persons, such as Mrs. A, want their pastor to take a definite "stand" on moral issues with convictions in counseling comparable to their pulpit proclamations. They have a rightful claim to this guidance but, in counseling, the pastor is cautioned to help them come to firm convictions of their own rather than to superficially impose his own upon them.

IN OPPOSITION TO ARTIFICIAL INSEMINATION

Many who oppose artificial insemination deem it inexpedient. They hold to the view that this procedure presents so many handicaps that it is likely to affect the child adversely, that it is expensive and inconvenient, and that it involves many complex ethical, legal and psychological problems. They contend that, at best, there are too many doubts to this procedure, and conclude, in the words of the Scripture, that "whatsoever does not proceed from faith is sin" (Romans 14:23).

Some strongly believe that both the obtaining of semen by masturbation and the means of their injection in artificial insemination is "unnatural" and immoral, an irreverent usurpation of the place, power and responsibility of the Creator. They maintain that the *only* means to pregnancy which is approved of God is "normal" sexual intercourse between husband and wife, that conception, as attested by the experiences of many childless couples, is not mandatory for marital oneness, strength and fulfillment, and that the injection in any way or means of a third party into a union intended for two only is sinful, and should, therefore, be opposed.

In donor insemination, some ministers reason that the living flesh of the donor's spermatozoon unites with the living flesh of the wife's ovum to produce a person who is a living testimony to a union which is other than the "one flesh" of husband and wife. Even when conception does not occur, the contact of donor semen with the genital tract of the wife is a union which violates that of husband and wife, and artificial insemination in which the semen of a donor and the semen of the husband are combined in the effort to effect pregnancy create an unholy trinity which cannot conform to the Scriptures which teach that "the two shall become one . . . What therefore God has joined together, let no man put asunder" (Matthew 19:5–6, RSV).

Many of those who oppose donor insemination feel that it cannot be reduced to an impersonal medical procedure for the couple when the objective is the birth of a "living soul"; thus they conclude that the use of donor semen not only precludes "impersonal objectivity" but also makes the procedure immoral.

The majority of those who oppose donor insemination believe that any violation of Christian ethic is also ultimately inexpedient, and, to their way of thinking, those who view donor insemination as a means of "semi-adoption" which brings happiness have a "near-sighted" perspective which does not comprehend the horizon of life-long effects upon the couple, the child, the donor, and, should they learn of the "donation," the donor's wife and children.

Legally, adultery implies sexual intercourse in which one of the parties is married to a third, and offspring from such illicit relations attests adultery. Those who seek legal action against artificial insemination reason that offspring by donor semen attests either to polygamy or to adultery, and both are illegal in America. They support their position further through the prevailing Christian interpretation of the Scripture which favors monogamy and opposes polygamy regardless of the fertility or infertility of the union. Some of those who strongly oppose donor insemination are crusading for law enforcement to abolish the "abominable" procedure, but the varying ethical views and conflictual social pressures are currently causing legislative leaders to avoid this "explosive" issue.

Many of those who oppose donor insemination do not, however, oppose artificial insemination when the husband's semen only is used. They feel that when the husband's semen is used exclusively, the "one flesh" union is not violated, the personal element is a helpful rather than a hindering factor, and the medical procedure is "therapeutic." As viewed by Roman Catholics, the entire procedure is "unnatural," even with the exclusive use of the husband's semen, but Protestant ethics voice no objection to the medical procedure when the husband's semen only is involved, and, pragmatically, the results support the means. Most Protestants thus conclude that artificial insemination by means of the exclusive use of the husband's semen is morally right and a helpful alternative which is preferable to childlessness.

CONCLUSIONS

The ethical concepts of the pastor significantly bear upon his ability to counsel those who are considering artificial insemination. While the needs of the couple may indicate that the convictions of the pastor should be sounded distinctly, coercion in counseling is inappropriate and harmful.

Lest the couple be confused in striving for the proper solution to their sterility problem, the facts of artificial insemination, both "pro and con," should be presented clearly in pastoral counseling, and the decision, together with its responsibility, should be left to the couple.

SEVEN

ADOPTION

Adoption is the best alternative for childless couples who desire, yet cannot have, children of their own.

In many instances couples assume, on the basis of years of fruitless efforts, that they are hopelessly sterile, and their first step in seeking aid comes with the decision to try to adopt a baby. They often bring their problem to the pastor for the first time when they seek information on where to go and how to proceed to adopt a baby. They may inquire of their pastor, as did Mr. and Mrs. L, "We've been thinking for a long time, and we've decided to adopt a baby, but we don't know how to go about it. We don't know where we should go, or what we should do, and we thought we'd come by to see if you could help us."

Of the 75,000 babies adopted annually in America, most go to the childless couples, but not all. Some couples with one or more children of their own seek to adopt another. Adoption is regarded with respect, and it does not bear a stigma sometimes associated with sterility. In contrast to communications regarding their infertility, many childless couples are able to discuss adoption quite freely. The pastor's efforts to counsel childless couples who seek adoption are thus enhanced.

In preparation for his referral ministry, the pastor should acquaint himself with the resources for adoption. Agencies which are not licensed and approved by the state should be avoided, and couples should be advised of the many complications, such as blackmail and legal entanglements, which can result when dealing with such racketeers. Couples are to be cautioned also against making "deals" with individuals who offer to sell their baby. With slight variations, numerous persons have had experiences similar to those of Mrs. R. An unwed, three-months pregnant woman told Mrs. R that she could have the baby when it was born providing that she pay all expenses incurred in connection with the pregnancy. Mrs. R trusted her, and paid all bills in full. When the baby was born the mother decided to keep her child, and she moved away without leaving a forwarding address. Mrs. R had only a verbal agreement, and no legal proceedings ensued.

The Children's Division of the Department of Public Welfare, State Department of Public Welfare, and local Council of Social Agencies which are licensed and approved may be recommended by the pastor. Complete information may be secured by writing to the Planned Parenthood Federation of America, Incorporated, 501 Madison Avenue, New York 22, New York. General information only, however, will not suffice in counseling the childless couple. They want to know specifically where to go, how to get there and what to expect. The pastor acts wisely who goes to local adoption agencies and secures first-hand information from social caseworkers as to local requirements and procedures.

Many childless couples approach an adoption agency for the first time with appreciable apprehension, and the pastor who goes "the second mile," time permitting, and accompanies them on this initial visit, strengthens the interpersonal relationships and renders a valuable service to the couple. His offer to accompany them will usually be accepted with deep gratitude and a sigh of relief.

Another initial question which most childless couples want to know is "what are our chances for adoption?" Prior to the first interview with a social caseworker of an adoption agency, the pastor can and should give the couple information which will bring their hope into conformity with reality. Due to the limited number of available children and to the existing requirements for adoption, only one of ten in America who make application for adoption are successful.[1] This statistical disadvantage will vary, favorably and unfavorably, from one local situation to another, but in almost all instances, there are far more applications than there are babies available for adoption. Although adoption is an excellent alternative to childlessness, the pastor is cautioned against offering unrealistic hope to couples who seek adoption. On the other hand, the pastor is not to paint such a dark picture that they lose patience and perseverance to pursue

[1] Ruth Carson, *So You Want To Adopt a Baby,* Public Affairs Pamphlet No. 173 (New York: Public Affairs Committee, Incorporated, 1951), p. 4.

this alternative when their only serious obstacle is quantitative rather than qualitative. The waiting period may be extremely long, but to those whose potential as parents is qualitatively "good," patient persistence is often rewarded by the desired adoption.

Before going to an adoption agency, many childless couples desire a general knowledge of what to expect in the procedure. The pastor helps to relieve their anxiety of the unknown by knowing and supplying this information. In applying for adoption, the couple, upon expressing their desire to adopt, are given a "preliminary application."

The initial information desired in the preliminary application to adopt a child usually concerns age, residence, employment and income, references, reasons for wanting a child by adoption, general marital history, physical description, reasons for not having their own children—with particular reference to fertility testing—and miscellaneous general information. Age is significant, because those who are over forty are generally considered too old to adopt a baby. Length of residence is a requirement as one indication of stability. Employment and income are important to the financial considerations for parenthood. References, particularly those of the pastor, family physician and lifelong acquaintances, are vital for a full and accurate study of the couple's home life.

In answering the question, "Why do you want to adopt a child?" the caseworkers of the adoption agency learn much about the couple's emotional aptitude for parenthood. There are many motives for adopting a child, but they may be reduced to two basic types: (1) motives which manipulate a child for selfish use, and (2) motives which value the child for, and of, himself. The emotional complex of motherliness is psychological and may be fulfilled in adoption, but the narcissistic "flesh of my flesh" pride is not so easily transferred. When such motivation predominates, one may expect to find a later sense of burden and disappointment. How the couple feel about being unable to have their own children indicates the extent of their narcissism and the ability to transfer tender care to another woman's child whom they wish to adopt.

A basic question in the preliminary application is, "Why not have a child of your own?" The childless couple should not be offended by the apparent presumptuousness of such a question as did sensitive Mrs. Y who exclaimed, "If I could have a baby of my own,

I certainly wouldn't be here now trying to adopt a baby. My husband and I have tried, and we just can't have a baby, that's all. I don't know why. Only God knows that, and I'm not God." Mrs. Y further stated that she would like to adopt a baby to give it a good home, just as she would her own, if she could have had a child. She had not sought fertility testing, and she saw no reason to do so.

The pastor reinforces his pastoral guidance by informing the couple that most adoption agencies require fertility examinations and medical statements of infertility prior to considering their application. This relatively recent requirement forces the couple, their pastor and the adoption agency to consider first the basic issue of sterility. The medical findings must indicate infertility, and the motives for desiring children must value a child for, and of, himself; otherwise, their applications are not considered.

One motive for adoption which some childless couples have when they seek to adopt is their hope that after adoption, the wife will then conceive and bear a child of her own. In a few instances, conception does occur after adoption, and these instances receive such widespread publicity that many have the popular misconception that adoption is the answer to fertility. The vast majority who adopt, however, never have children of their own, and such a motive is both negative and unfounded.

In the preliminary application, a general marital history is important to note the length of the present marriage, previous marriages and children of any marriage. Physical descriptions are needed to "match" the adopted baby to the couple in physical characteristics. If previous applications have been made, or if other applications are presently before another agency, then this will also have a bearing upon the success of the application.

Following the preliminary application, it is usually required that the couple undergo a physical examination. This examination includes medical history, blood tests, chest x-ray, urinalysis and confirmation of infertility together with an overall picture of general health.

After the adoption agency receives the medical report and the preliminary application, an appointment is made for an interview with a social caseworker. All records and information are strictly confidential and highly personal, and before placing a baby in a home for adoption, all aspects of the adoptive parents' lives are thoroughly explored. The likelihood of keeping anything that is relevant hidden is highly improbable, and couples who have a "hidden past" are cautioned against efforts to deceive. From the very beginning, couples who apply for adoption should be conditioned to communicate freely, conceal nothing and cooperate fully.

With the first interview by the social caseworker, indoctrination begins. Some agencies present booklets to adoptive applicants which answer many questions on procedure and possibilities. Instruction and information is an integral part of the several conferences with the social worker assigned to the case and within group meetings. Additionally, some agencies either require or "highly recommend" that couples read such books as Louise Raymond's *Adoption and After* (New York: Harper & Row, Publishers, 1955, 238 pages) and such public affairs pamphlets as Ruth Carson's *So You Want to Adopt a Baby* (Number 173, *op. cit.*, 32 pages). An extensive bibliography will include publications by the Planned Parenthood Federation of America, the American Medical Society, the Public Affairs Committee, Incorporated, and state agencies. The indoctrination prepares the couple both for receiving the child and for rearing the child after adoption.

The adoptive procedure continues with several interviews. The social caseworker may "stop by" unannounced, without an appointment, on several occasions, or all home visits may be made by appointment only, depending upon the local policies. In addition to interviewing the couple who have applied for adoption, the social worker may interview the pastor, family physician and references. In some instances, letters of reference are all that is needed or desired, but whether the pastor is interviewed or called upon for a letter of reference, or both, his responsibility is great and his judgment is highly valued. He is concerned for the best welfare of the child as well as for the childless couple. He does not desire to be instrumental in closing the door to those who, though not presently "good prospects," could probably make a satisfactory adjustment through counseling. Neither does he desire that the couple adopt a child before they have resolved their infertility trauma. In such instances, he can indicate to the agency the potential of the couple and recommend that judgment be suspended temporarily, and that the decision be held in abeyance for a designated period of time. In each instance, his convictions and the facts upon which he bases his convictions are indicated, and, despite his intentions and efforts to help, he does no one a favor when he prejudices his position.

Prior to the resolution of the infertility trauma, involuntarily childless couples are poor candidates for adoption. Only as the trauma is faced and fathomed is it healed, and this usually requires from six months to two years from the date of discovery. Couples who refuse to accept the fact of infertility, who do not know that they are sterile until after the required medical examinations and fertility testing of the adoption process, or who fail to face and to work through their infertility problem, are not emotionally ready to begin the steps in applying for adoption. The psychological aptitude for treating an adopted child as their own is in direct proportion to the extent to which both the husband and wife have "faced" and resolved their sterility trauma. This obviously calls for pastoral counseling on a long-term basis before beginning the process of adoption in a relationship which enables the couple to mourn their fertility loss, to explore the theological, ethical and emotional roots of their problem and to re-affirm the Godly way of life to the limit of their humanity.

The pastor is cautioned that mere suggestions to the barren couple that they consult a social worker of a specific adoption agency is grossly inadequate. An attitude of responsible and helpful concern is prerequisite to meaningful pastoral referral. The pastor may logically conclude that he can best help infertile couples who seek adoption by first confronting with them the problem of sterility and by enlisting all available resources to meet their multi-dimensional needs. Not only should the pastor make meaningful referrals, but also he should supportively follow the step by step progress of these couples throughout and following the adoption process. Couples feel neglected when referred prematurely and "dropped." Furthermore, the pastor misses excellent opportunities to minister to the spiritual needs which are created, or cultivated, by their sterility trauma.

Mr. G, age 32, U.S. Army, was sterilized by atomic radiation. He became morose, bitter and exceedingly sensitive. His chaplain expressed sincere sympathy, but Mr. G refused to "face the issue." Six months later Mr. and Mrs. G contacted their chaplain concerning adoption. She, age 28, fertile, expressed some resentment of his condition. He began to communicate his sense of loss. The chaplain recommended that they wait a few months longer to get better adjusted to the idea of sterility before attempting to adopt. He invited

them to his home for a visit. The couple came, and that was the beginning of some ten or eleven informal visits. Communication became progressively better. The chaplain and Mr. G "strolled around"
outside and talked, while Mrs. G and the chaplain's wife were in the
kitchen discussing Mrs. G's problems over a cup of coffee. Motives
for adoption were discussed until both Mr. and Mrs. G came to an
unselfish appreciation of a child as a person. The chaplain and his
wife privately compared "notes." Eight months from the date of their
first informal visit the chaplain went with Mr. and Mrs. G to see a
social caseworker of a reputable adoption agency. Their application
was approved, and eleven months later they adopted a one-year-old
boy. The boy is now nine, and the three of them feel that they belong
to each other as if the child were their own "flesh and blood."

An informal, permissive relationship may be essential to establish
the needful rapport for pastoral care in counseling. Prior to the resolution of the sterility trauma, adoption may be symbolic of disappointment and similar to "rebound" marriages. The emotional complex of motherliness may be fulfilled in adoption when the narcissistic
motivation is secondary and subordinate. The pastor thus seeks the
full resolution of the sterility trauma prior to referring the couple to
the social caseworker of an adoption agency.

When the pastor is called upon for a reference, he needs to
know the couple's motives for adoption, their degree of acceptance
of their sterility and their ability to give adequate, loving care to a
child. As couples come to the pastor for referral, he may further communication by stating that he will probably be consulted as a reference and, in such a capacity, thus needs the above-mentioned, additional information.

From the date of the first visit in the home of the childless
couple by the social caseworker, a definite time limit is set by most
agencies for the completion of the "home studies," the interviewing
of references and the review of the application. Six months or longer
may be anticipated from the time of starting to the time of culminat-
ing the interviews of the application process; then the applicants are
usually notified that a definite decision has been reached. These
months are characterized by uncertainty and are plagued with apprehension; thus, in similarity to the diagnostic period of fertility
testing, the pastor's function in counseling includes supportive reassurance, and, even when these couples are notified that their appli-

cation is rejected, a sense of relief accompanies the termination of this period of doubt.

When the applications for adoption are approved, these couples are placed on a "waiting list" until the baby that is "right" for each couple in physical features is available. This period of waiting, which is dependent upon the number of approved applications and upon the number of available babies, may extend from months into years. The pastor who "stands by" them faithfully throughout this extended time of tension and who counsels them in their moments of sagging patience and "blue" depression is a valuable and cherished shepherd of the flock. He may realistically reassure these couples that their applications would not have been accepted had they not been flexible, mature and, in contrast to sensitive egocentrics, warmly "outgoing" human beings who were esteemed as strong enough to persevere patiently and to endure steadfastly the unavoidable delays. This affirmation of confidence tends to beget confidence both in themselves and the agency and, subsequently, stimulates renewed contentment in hope for the ultimate reward of a baby of their own.

The next step in the adoption procedure occurs on the happy day when the applicants are notified that the agency has a baby that they want the couple to see. The couple come to the agency, and they are often left alone with the baby for as long as they desire to stay; then a social caseworker answers some of their questions. For instance, to queries about childhood diseases, a medical history of the baby is given, and to questions concerning family background, the social worker can state the type of background but cannot reveal specific and identifying information. If the couple then want the baby that was shown to them, they are instructed by a medical staff member in infant and child care. They learn, for instance, such important things as how to prepare the baby's formula, how to bathe and clothe the baby, how to maintain or to cultivate good sleeping habits and how to cope properly with a rapidly growing personality. A formal and legal agreement with the adoption agency which states the terms of placement and supervision is signed; then the baby may be taken "home." The ministry of the pastor is indicated on the same basis as that for any couple who have a "new" baby in the home.

The first year, or the period agreed upon for supervision, of the adoption is regarded as a "confirmation" rather than a "probation" period. The agency has confidence in the couple, otherwise, they do not place a baby in their home. The period of time agreed upon is for the confirmation of convictions by experience, and is not a "trial" period which gambles experimentally with the precious life of a helpless infant. In similarity to other couples with their first child, adoptive parents will make mistakes and become tired, irritated and distressed. Adoptive parents are not expected to be perfect. That they react "normally" and without gross or extended deviations from the "norm" is sufficient. To relieve the tension of the couple which is created by fear of making a mistake, the pastor with a sense of humility and humor may relate an incident of his fallibility as a father (if, indeed, he is a father, for unquestionably he is fallible!), laugh with the couple at himself, and conclude that by the grace of God they "survived" and "adjusted well" despite human frailties. Blessed is the pastor from whom these adoptive parents can learn by identification with him to let God be God, to let man be man and to let there be no confusion of the two in person, role, function and sovereign-subordinate relationship.

The last steps in the process of adoption are legal. Each state has statutes concerning adoption, and the variations from state to state are minor. In some states, after the child has been placed in the home for approximately six months, the adoptive couple may file a Petition for Adoption and support this petition by documents from the adoption agency. Custody of the child to the adoptive parents on a provisional basis is then issued by the Superior Court holding the petition by means of an Interlocutory Decree. After the child has lived for one year and a day with the adoptive parents, the Final Order of Adoption may be issued; then the adoption is completed, and the child belongs to the adoptive parents with "no strings attached," just as though he were their own "flesh and blood" heir and offspring. Some couples approach legal proceedings with fear and trembling, but the laws of adoption cast a long shadow of comfort rather than of fear for the adoptive parents. These laws are designed to protect the baby and the adoptive parents, and to prevent disturbances or disruptions in adoptive homes from relatives of the baby and from all "outside" sources. Armed in counseling with such information and interpretations, the couple who adopt may approach the legal aspects of adoption with confidence and gratitude. The pastor, acquainted with the statutes of his State on adoption, is thus in a better position to counsel adoptive parents at this point in the developmental process.

Counseling the childless couple does not end with the Final Order of Adoption. The pastor will be concerned that the home adjustments be characterized by love, acceptance, mutual appreciation, security and Christian education. The pastoral heart desires that the child grows as did Jesus who "increased in wisdom and in stature, and in favor with God and man" (Luke 2:52). Religion and membership "in good standing" of a local church, to insure spiritual growth of the adopted child, are significant considerations of the social agency in the placement of a child in the home, and the pastor desires that the religious bonds be strengthened and lengthened. A superficial religion, however, used as a means of manipulation, will probably be slackened and shortened after the couple achieve their desired objective of adoption. That the couple's religion be genuine and dynamic is vital to the Christian home (Psalm 127:1). The pastor also encourages the couple to be honest with the child by telling him at an early age that he is adopted, loved, wanted, regarded as fully their own and treasured dearly, and the pastor recommends that the couple demonstrate these truths by rearing the child like any other child.

The results of such counseling of the truly parental couple are gratifying. The narcissistic pride of the couple is transferred in a few months to the child, and the baby becomes a genuine and indistinguishable part of themselves.

Adoption brings many changes, and one of the most "mysterious" and "miraculous" in the concept of the couple is conception after adoption. Formerly, when fertility tests were not a prerequisite to adoption, many pastors recall instances of fertility after adoption. To seek adoption to aid fertility is, however, a negative motive which the pastor seeks to correct. Under existing requirements of many agencies, which require complete and competent fertility testing both of the husband and the wife, fertility after adoption is improbable, though not impossible. A few couples who are relatively infertile may, after adoption, fully accept childlessness, experience relief from fear and guilt, and conceive. The pastor who understands phychogenic sterility may lead the couple in counseling to new and positive emotional experiences and attitudes which release the body from fertility blockage. To further the pastor's insight and understanding and, thereby, to further his ability to counsel the childless couple, the following instances of fertility after adoption are offered.

Mrs. Z, age 32, desired children so intensely that coitus became excessive, compulsive and repulsive. Vaginismus, the constriction of the vagina which prevents coitus, resulted from her apprehensive excitement and negative approach. Following adoption, she "relaxed." Her inner inhibitions were removed by the fulfillment of adoption, and with this motivation change, her vaginal constrictions ceased. She later became pregnant.

Mrs. Y, age 28, had been married to Mr. Y, age 26, for eight years. During the first few years of marriage she regarded him as immature in every respect, and the thoughts of his becoming a father of her child frightened her; then Mr. Y expressed concern for a child and insisted that if they could not have one of their own, they should adopt. They did adopt, and Mr. Y proved to be emotionally ready for fatherhood. Mrs. Y gained confidence in her husband, lost her inhibitions concerning him and progressively "relaxed." Two years after adoption she conceived.

Mrs. X, age 30, was the victim of morbid feelings of guilt. She felt that since she had sinned in pre-marital sexual experiences that she was doomed to childlessness, that happiness within marriage was "not intended" for her and that it was impossible for her to atone for her sins. Mr. X, age 34, wanted a son. They adopted a baby boy and became very happy as parents. Experience disproved her theory. She gained hope of happiness in every aspect of life. She lost the morbid tenseness of self-punishment, and conceived when she was 33.

Mrs. W, age 35, was a "career woman," an executive of prestige, influence and wealth. She was as conscientiously determined to advance as any man in the firm. Her mother taught her by precept and example to abhor motherhood and "housework," and encouraged her to get out "in the world" and be "free like a man." That she did, but her love for her husband led her to doubt this philosophy of life. She then tried to give her husband a child, but could not. They later adopted a child. She found that her fears and revulsions were unfounded, and that motherhood had many rewarding experiences. Psychologically, she came to accept femininity and motherhood, then she became pregnant.

Mrs. V, age 27, led a sheltered life. From early childhood she had been told repeatedly, "You can't do that. Here, let me do it." She was neither taught to accept responsibility nor given the opportunity to learn to manage for herself in her childhood home. She felt so inferior that she feared that she would not be able to care for a child properly. "I don't think that I'd make a good mother," she said in voicing a deep-seated conviction of hers. Mr. V, age 33, had confidence in his wife, and he complimented her on her every achievement, regardless of how minor it was. They tried to have children "for his sake," but failed. With his promise to help her with the baby, they sought and obtained a baby by adoption. He "kept his word," but with each passing month, she gained confidence by the proof of performance, and she "called on him for help" less and less. She lost her feelings of inferiority, grew to evaluate her abilities realistically, accepted the femininity of maturity and became pregnant.

In each of these instances, fear and worry enslaved the body and prevented fertility; then, when fear and guilt were discharged, confidence was gained, reconciliations to roles were made, and love was expressed without antagonism, ambivalence, or restraint, and the wives became fertile.

GROUP GUIDANCE

In addition to group guidance as previously indicated to prevent sterility, the pastor may effectively guide groups of infertile couples to wholesome adjustments to their sterility trauma. The pastor may entitle the group study "Alternatives to Childlessness," and include discussions on adoption, artificial insemination by the husband's semen and medical diagnosis and treatment which facilitate fertility. In churches which support orphanages, the study of, and concern for, homeless children and adoption is an honor rather than a stigma. Homeless children also come as a result of separation, desertion, divorce, court action and illness, and are welfare situations which merit group studies of Public Welfare needs and which necessitate the enlistment of couples who will serve as foster parents on a temporary basis. Pastors have many excellent opportunities for group guidance of infertile couples in discussions on adoption and foster parents.

A number of childless ministers, with whom the writer is acquainted, take a keen interest in adoption and in the support of orphanages. They guide groups in these studies, and many of them are now adoptive parents. Properly guided, many groups of childless couples may find, through discussions on adoption, a positive solution to their sterility problem.

Numerous churches contribute to orphanages and also sponsor

individual children of these orphanages. Group discussions which indoctrinate the church membership on such things as requirements for admission to children's homes, policies and procedures of specific orphanages and the availability of the children of the orphanage for adoption are a needful, if not integral, part of the educational program of the church. Such discussions may logically serve as a springboard for discussions on infertility. At such group meetings, infertile couples may initiate and plan informal discussions in the home with other childless couples who revealed similar problems and needs by the questions which they asked in the group indoctrination on orphanages.

As illustrated by the group meetings of infertile couples who register for treatment at the Margaret Sanger Research Bureau in New York, group guidance can be utilized very advantageously. Six or eight of the two hundred childless couples registered comprise one group. The initial "orientation session" is a lecture by a doctor on the male and female reproductive system and the basic essentials of fertility. Time is then devoted to answering the specific questions of the group. Subsequent group meetings give less time to lecturing and more time for informal discussion of mutual problems. Permissive discussion of infertility and other mutual problems is encouraged, and the staff member who is "in charge" of the group unobtrusively keeps the conversation moving "on course." Approximately one-third of the two hundred couples gained reassurance from these group discussions, experienced release from anxiety and other tensions and rejoiced in the group "therapy" which resulted in pregnancy. One month after attending the first group meeting, one wife reported that she had not menstruated, and pregnancy was later confirmed. All of the couples profited by being a part of the group. Upon seeing other intelligent, healthy persons with similar fears and needs, these couples realize that they are not alone, and are relieved of much of their anxiety.

Group guidance is excellent "therapy" for the anxiety of loneliness. Counseling one person at a time has many merits, but individual counseling does not and cannot cope with loneliness as effectively as group guidance. For maximum benefits the pastor should, therefore, counsel both individuals and groups of childless couples. The group experiences of those at the Margaret Sanger Research Bureau may show the pastor not only what can be done, but also how to structure the group in his church for effective guidance. Although the pastor may initiate a group study of adoption, he may discover that various persons within the group wish to discuss other alternatives to childlessness. He may thus find it advantageous to subdivide the group by age, background, intelligence and specialized interests.

The writer concludes, therefore, that group guidance is potentially a strong resource which, though previously only partially realized, can and should be utilized in the pastoral care of the childless couple.

THOSE WHO REMAIN CHILDLESS

(1) Those who are involuntarily childless yet who reject all alternatives, (2) those who desire to adopt but cannot and (3) those who voluntarily choose childlessness are the three major groups of childless couples yet to be considered.

When the wife is absolutely sterile, or when, excluding artificial insemination, polygamy, infidelity and divorce, the husband is permanently sterile, the alternatives for the couple are either childlessness or adoption. Some couples prefer childlessness to adoption because they feel that if they cannot have a child of their own, then they had rather have none.

> Mrs. Q was permanently sterile. Her husband's vocation kept him away from home about 50 percent of the time. She was a first grade school teacher, and she was attached to these children. They felt that a child would necessitate a change or alteration in vocation for both of them which they did not desire. They both were narcissistic to the point of rejecting a child unless he were their own. Mrs. Q said, "I want a baby, but if I can't have one of my own by my own husband, I'd rather have none at all." They were well adjusted vocationally, and well respected in the church and in the community. Their problem was solved to their satisfaction, and the pastor made no effort to dissuade them from their views on adoption.

What percentage of childless couples comprise this group is not known, but the probability is that, while there are a multitude of couples who apply for adoption, there are far more who would like to have children of their own but who make no effort toward securing a child by other means from another source. Only from first-hand knowledge of the childless couples will the pastor know who "fits" into this local category. Pastoral counseling is indicated to counteract hyper-narcissism even apart from considerations of fertility and paternity.

A second group of couples who remain childless permanently are the absolutely sterile who desire adoption but who, for one reason or another, are unable to adopt. Many couples, for instance, keep procrastinating in the hope that they will yet have children of their own, and do not seek adoption until they are too old to be considered.

> Mrs. O, age 50, stated that she had never discussed her problem of childlessness with her pastor "until now." She told him that she went to the "Welfare Department" "a few years ago" to try to adopt a baby and was told that she exceeded the age limit. She said, "I guess it was God's will for me to have no children. I don't know. It hurts terribly bad, worse than anything else in the world. The older I get, the worse it hurts, and the more I wish for children of my own." Mr. O, age 58, stated that he always wanted a son of his own but that he guessed it was "hopeless now . . . age is against us." The pastor led them from speculations about the past to consideration of God's will for the present and future. Even though there were no alternatives to childlessness, the pastor voiced his vision of their ample opportunities to be with and to influence the children of the community. They claimed that vision of hope, and two years later, all the children in the church and in the community were calling them "Aunt" and "Uncle," and clamoring for their attention, affection, delicious pastries and "treats" of various sorts. In these relationships, Mr. and Mrs. O found happiness and a sense of achievement. They experienced compensations because, as Mr. O told his pastor, "In a way we feel as though we have had children. We baby-sit, and we have children around us so much that they seem like our own . . . at least for a little while, and that's a lot better than nothing."

Such childless couples as Mr. and Mrs. O have no alternatives to childlessness. They are permanently sterile, and would not, therefore, profit by either divorce or artificial insemination. They can neither adopt nor become foster parents. Many couples, such as Mr. and Mrs. O, bear witness to lost opportunities in counseling the childless couple. Pastoral counseling is needful for sterile couples of all ages, and the earlier the problem is met, the more favorable the prognosis for spiritual fulfillment and for parenthood.

Low income and irregular employment of the husband may bar the door to adoption.

Mr. H, age 33, was a carpenter's helper. He was an unskilled laborer whose employment was seasonal. During off-seasons he was a jack-of-all-trades in order to have enough money to pay his debts. Mrs. H, age 29, was permanently sterile. She and her husband loved children, and children enjoyed being with them. They sought to adopt a child but were refused for financial reasons. Highly offended, Mr. H said, "I can't help it if I ain't had an education so's I could get a good-paying job. I don't see why that should be held against a man. I know lots of families that are poor as snakes, but they make out all right because they love each other. Maybe I couldn't buy the kid the best clothes or afford to send him to the best schools, but I could love him, and, as I see it, that's all that really matters." Mr. H later secured permanent employment at $1.25 per hour in a textile plant and could then have applied again for adoption, but he was "through with those ———— people at that place." Knowing their love for children and their current circumstances, the pastor recommended to proper authorities that they be considered for temporary placement of "welfare cases" in their home. Three months later they became foster parents. The first child, a six-month-old boy, they kept until he was three. A second child, a two-year-old girl, was placed in the home when the boy was eighteen months old. They have had from one to three such children in their home ever since. Mr. and Mrs. H told their pastor, "We feel that we are helping out, and at the same time we're profiting in two ways. We're getting paid for keeping these children, and we're enjoying being 'mama' and 'papa.'" Both Mr. and Mrs. H were from "big families" of several brothers and sisters, and they voiced another feeling of compensation: "You know, it's a good feeling to have such a 'big family' of your own, even if you don't get to keep them with you very long. A lot of folks we talk to tell us that 'it seems only yesterday since our children were babies, and now they're out from underfoot and gone.'"

Securing children as foster parents even on a temporary basis is an alternative which offers far more than is readily apparent, and, as indicated, the pastor does well to explore the possibilities of this alternative with involuntarily childless couples who desire to adopt but cannot.

Some who apply for adoption are disqualified because they do not meet the requirements of physical health.

When Mrs. H was 22, one year after marriage, she was seriously injured in an auto accident. Her hip and spine were broken, and her doctor informed her that pregnancy might prove fatal; thus, he advised sterilization by surgery. She consented, and the operation was performed. Thereafter, at best, she walked with difficulty and, at worst, she was "bedfast." When she enjoyed improved health, she was frequently called upon by her brother to baby-sit with his sons, ages 3 and 5. She sometimes kept them for as long as six hours at a time. She managed this by keeping them in the house and by supervising their play while sitting. Then, at the age of 32, she decided that she could "manage a baby" with her husband's help, and she sought to adopt. For health reasons her application was rejected. She continued to baby-sit, and she often told her pastor about her "two boys" who seemed as much like her own as they did her brother's, and she was pleased that they "turned to her" and her husband in times of need as quickly as they did to their own mother and daddy.

With the increasing number of "working mothers" and the shortage of reputable and reliable "baby sitters," this is an alternative which, apparently, is continuous for the truly motherly-type of childless wives. Such bonds can become so strong that both the childless wife and the child come to think of the baby sitter as the "second mom." The same can hold true of the infertile husband who frequently "takes care of the boys" for relatives or friends. He becomes their "second dad." Church, school and community activities also offer many other intimate experiences with children. Those couples who truly desire the experience of belonging in relationships with children thus have many opportunities for a "taste" or "touch" of parenthood, and, if the axiom is true that "it is better to have loved and lost than never to have loved at all," then it is better to experience a type of parenthood even on a temporary basis than to insist upon "all or nothing at all." The pastor's task in counseling is not to "push" children upon the childless couple. Rather, it is to indicate the manifold alternatives and opportunities together with their advantages and disadvantages in an effort to help them to achieve maximum personal fulfillment. The decision as to which of the many roads to travel is a sacred right and responsibility of the couple and is respected and preserved without encroachment by the discerning counselor.

Those who voluntarily choose childlessness are the third and last group of childless couples to be considered. In view of specialized vocations which require extensive education, training, research or travel, coupled with a serious regard for the constantly increasing

problem of overpopulation, some childless couples voluntarily re-
nounce parenthood for wholehearted dedication to a specialized vocational "calling" which they believe is vital to today's predicaments
and, therefore, approved of God. They eliminate all non-essential
responsibilities and distractions, and pursue their vocation with a
religious dedication. Rather than to dissuade such couples from their
chosen and childless vocation, the pastor's concern is that their sub-
merged emotions and motivations match the surfaced logic of their
mind, and that they accept or reject parenthood on a mature, responsible and ethical vocational basis.

Other couples soberly and excessively affirm that they do not
desire children of their own, that they are fully content to leave parenthood to others, and that the best life for them is the childless life;
whereas, in actuality, they may fear parenthood to the extent of
"pushing the thoughts out of their mind" into the unconscious and
"coming up with" the rationalization that they did not want children
after all. They may be like the paranoid who thought, "I love you;
you hate me; therefore, I hate you." They may actually have a serious
sterility problem and not be consciously aware of it. The veteran
counselor also listens with "the third ear," and excesses of affirma-
tions and negations, as well as what is left "unsaid," warn him against
gullible acceptance of all statements at "face value." Painful as it may
be, the pastor renders his best counseling ministry when he helps
such couples to see, accept, confront and resolve their sterility trauma.

The godly pastor accepts childless couples where they are rather
than where he wants them to be. He perceives the potential and the
specific needs of each individual. He loves, forgives, accepts and seeks
for them new and abundant life rather than condemnation and destruction. He takes them forward one step and one day at a time, yet
he does not lose sight of the ultimate goal of filling their cup of life
with love and faith until it overflows. As the pastor relates to childless couples in the Spirit of Christ, his ministry will be blessed because it is "in His name" and in keeping with His character.

Statistically, the possibilities for resolving the infertility problem
in the near future are as follows: over 50 percent of those who are
childless can, by means of thorough medical diagnosis and competent
treatment, have their own child; 10 percent can adopt; 1 percent
may qualify psychologically for artificial insemination by donor
semen; 5 percent may become foster parents "for a season"; 20 percent

may conscientiously and religiously elect a vocational "calling" without parenthood; then less than 14 percent remain to mourn and be comforted, to come to accept the permanent vocation of "spiritual" parenthood only through their contacts with and influence over children of others.

From a developmental approach as followed in this writing, the care of the pastor in counseling the childless couple nears completion. This is illustrated by those couples who have mourned their loss, worked through a multitude of anxieties, and considered various alternatives. When the final door of alternatives is closed, however, and the couple must remain childless throughout life, a rending of old wounds of grief is experienced. That they be comforted and that they find life meaningful in Christ are objectives which can be achieved in counseling under the leadership of the Holy Spirit.

EIGHT

SUMMARY And CONCLUSIONS

1. Couples who are involuntarily childless over an extended period of time have a sterility problem. To determine the extent of the sterility problem, the pastor should learn the parental desires of the couples under his spiritual care who are childless after two or more years of marriage.

2. The initial tasks of the pastor who ministers to the sterile and, thus, childless couple are (1) to promote communication, (2) to correct their theological misconception of God's will and purposes of marriage, (3) to explore their emotional roots of self-diagnosis, (4) to reassure them realistically and (5) to refer them to their family physician.

3. During the comprehensive diagnostic survey, the pastor supports the childless couple by meeting their needs for (1) emotional release, (2) information, (3) reassurance and (4) patience. This he does most effectively by timely and appropriate use of the religious resources, especially of the Scriptures and of prayer.

4. As the couple learn the cause or causes of their sterility, they experience anxieties of grief, guilt, hostility, inferiority, loneliness and finitude, and thus need pastoral counseling in a controlled relationship for several weeks. Comfort from grief, confession of sin, reconciliation to God and a new vocational perspective under God are vital needs which the pastor endeavors to meet while counseling the childless couple.

5. The pastor should note the similarities and differences between Scriptural and contemporary attitudes toward sterility, and, by the use of the Bible in counseling, lead the couple to identify with sterile persons of the Scriptures whose attitudes are positive.

6. Pastoral counseling is essential to a favorable spiritual prognosis of the childless couple, and is a potent aid to conception and

subsequent parenthood. The pastor ministers to the individual, to the couple and to groups, both to prevent and to resolve the sterility problem.

7. As the barren couple come to pray realistically, intelligently, maturely and effectively, and as they come to walk with God in keeping with answered prayer, the pastoral counseling of the childless couple is most commendable.

8. *Theological conclusions.* (1) The will of God for a childless couple is maximum life within their God-given humanity, which is not to be presupposed, but is to be determined logically and prayerfully on the foundation of facts. The will of God in childlessness may not, therefore, be known prior to competent medical diagnosis. God is consistent and impartial, and those who conform to his physiological laws of fertility can have children of their own, and this principle is operative regardless of the personal merits and demerits of any couple. (2) The essential purpose of marriage is unitive, and is fulfilled despite the presence or absence of children. Sterility does not negate conjugal rights, and is not ethically significant to sexual intercourse in marriage. (3) Experiential knowledge verifies the possibility of human fulfillment for husbands and wives of childless unions. The emotion of motherliness, for example, may be fulfilled in adoption. Becoming foster parents, teaching children in public, private, parochial and church schools, working with children in various church groups or activities and baby-sitting are some of the many other experiential means to parental fulfillment, and, even though they are temporary, they offer many compensations. As Abraham became the spiritual father of many Gentiles, so can an infertile husband become the spiritual father of many children in, for example, his work with boys of the church and community.

9. *Ethical and moral conclusions.* (1) The pastor errs when he forsakes his religious role, when he egotistically and solitarily seeks to meet the total needs of the childless couple, when he refers these couples without first ministering to their spiritual needs, and when he neglects his stewardship in the use of the religious resources of pastoral counseling. (2) Sterilization for self-preservation and for some eugenic purposes is morally right. (3) Divorce for childlessness is sinful, and should be opposed by the Christian pastor. (4) Out of the "heart" proceed the basic ethical and moral issues of artificial in-

semination by donor semen. Mark 7:21 and Matthew 5:28 are solid Scriptural supports for this conclusion. Despite the tremendously logical and practical appeal, ethical conclusions which are based upon technicalities and expediency in contending either for or against artificial insemination are not valid. Artificial insemination by the husband's semen only is ethically approved as a therapeutic medical procedure. (5) Masturbation for the purposes of fertility testing and for artificial insemination by the husband's semen when medically indicated is needful, or therapeutic, and morally approved. (6) Sins which are directly associated with sterility are illicit sexual relations in which sterilizing venereal diseases are contracted, abuse of general health, induced abortion and idolatrous desires for children which cause psychogenic sterility. Not all sterility is a result of sin. Regardless of the cause of infertility, the pastor does not condemn; instead, he seeks to lead the individual to maximum fulfillment through repentance, reconciliation to God and a life which abides and abounds in Christ. (7) Couples are morally obligated to seek or to avoid conception as eugenic, personal, psychological, time, economic, environmental and other such factors indicate under the prayerful guidance of the Holy Spirit.

APPENDIX A

BIBLIOGRAPHY

A. BOOKS

BUXTON, CHARLES L., and ANNA L. SOUTHAM. *Human Infertility.* New York: Harper & Row, Publishers, 1958. 229 pp.

DUVALL, EVELYN MILLIS. *Facts of Life and Love for Teen-Agers.* New York: Popular Library, 1957. 304 pp.

EPSTEIN, LOUIS M. *Sex Laws and Customs in Judaism.* New York: Block Publishing Company, 1948. 251 pp.

FISHBEIN, MORRIS. *Children for the Childless: A Concise Explanation of the Medical, Scientific, and Legal Facts about Conception, Fertility, Sterility, Heredity, and Adoption.* First edition, Garden City: Doubleday and Company, Inc., 1954. 223 pp.

FORSDIKE, SIDNEY. *Sterility in Women: Diagnosis and Treatment.* London: H. K. Lewis and Company, 1952. 18 pp.

GALTON, LAWRENCE N. *New Facts for the Childless.* New York: Thomas Y. Crowell Company, 1953. 184 pp.

GRIFFITH, EDWARD F. *Childless Marriage: Its Causes and Cure.* Revised edition of *Childless Family: Its Causes and Cure.* London: Methuen and Company, Ltd., 1948. 218 pp.

HAMBLEN, EDWIN C. *Facts for Childless Couples.* Revised fourth printing, Springfield, Ill.: Charles C Thomas, Publisher, 1950. 110 pp.

MACE, DAVID R. *Hebrew Marriage: A Sociological Study.* London: The Epworth Press, 1953. 291 pp.

MEAD, MARGARET. *Male and Female: A Study of the Sexes in a Changing World.* Fourth printing, New York: William Morrow and Company, 1950. 477 pp.

OATES, WAYNE E. *Where to Go for Help.* Philadelphia: The Westminster Press, 1957. 118 pp.

ROMMER, J. JAY. *Sterility: Its Causes and Its Treatment.* Springfield, Ill.: Charles C Thomas, 1952. 425 pp.

RUBIN, ISADOR C. *Uterotubal Insufflation: A Clinical Diagnostic Method of Determining the Tubal Factor in Sterility.* St. Louis: G. V. Mosby Company, 1947. 453 pp.

SIEGLER, SAMUEL L. *Fertility in Women: Causes, Diagnosis and Treatment of Impaired Fertility.* Philadelphia: J. B. Lippincott Company, 1944. 450 pp.

STONE, ABRAHAM, and HANNAH STONE. *A Marriage Manual: A Practical Guidebook to Sex and Marriage.* New York: Simon and Schuster, 1952. 301 pp.

VELDE, THEODOOR HENRICK VAN DE. *Fertility and Sterility in Marriage: Their Voluntary Promotion and Limitation.* New York: Covici, Friede, Medical Books, 1931. 448 pp.

WEISMAN, ABNER I. *Spermatozoa and Sterility: A Clinical Manual.* New York: Hoeber Medical Div., Harper & Row, Publishers, 1941. 314 pp.

B.   SERIES AND ARTICLES IN COLLECTIONS

DEUTSCH, HELENE. *Psychology of Women: A Psychoanalytic Interpretation.* 2 vols., New York: Grune and Stratton, 1944.

C.   PUBLICATIONS OF THE GOVERNMENT, LEARNED SOCIETIES AND OTHER ORGANIZATIONS

CARSON, RUTH. *So You Want to Adopt a Baby.* (Public Affairs Pamphlet No. 173.) New York: Public Affairs Committee, Incorporated, 1951. 32 pp.

D.   PERIODICALS

BAYER, LEONA M. "Potential Infertility in Young Women: Medical Alertness vs. Patient Anxiety," *Fertility and Sterility.* 5(5):461–67, September–October, 1954.

BICKERS, WILLIAM. "Uterine Contraction Patterns: Effects of Psychic Stimuli on the Myometrium," *Fertility and Sterility.* 7(3):268–75, May–June, 1956.

BLAKESLEE, ALTON L. "Emotional Block," *Today's Health.* 32:14–15, October, 1954.

BOX, CARLO, and R. A. CLEGHORN. "Psychogenic Sterility," *Fertility and Sterility.* 9(2):85–90, March–April, 1958.

BUXTON, CHARLES LEE (ed.). "Artificial Insemination: Genetic, Legal, and Ethical Implications: A Symposium," *Fertility and Sterility*. 9(4):368–75, July–August, 1958.

———. "The Presence of an 'X' Factor or Factors as a Cause of Human Sterility," *Fertility and Sterility*. 2(6):545–46, November–December, 1951.

FISHER, N. K., and C. T. BEECHAM. "Some Psychosomatic Obstetric and Gynecologic Problems," *West Virginia Medical Journal*. 54(4):119–24, April, 1958.

FORD, E. S., and I. FORMAN. "A Psychodynamic Approach to the Study of Infertility," *Fertility and Sterility*. 4(6):456–65, November–December, 1953.

GAMBLE, CLARENCE J. "Why Fear Sterilization?" *Hygeia*. 26:20–60, January, 1948.

GOSNEY, E. S. "Twenty-eight Years of Eugenic Sterilization in California," *Eugenic News*. 22:86–87, September–October, 1937.

HULME, HAROLD B. "Effect of Semistarvation on Human Semen," *Fertility and Sterility*. 2(4):319–31, July–August, 1951.

JACOBSON, EDITH. "A Case of Sterility," *The Psychoanalytic Quarterly*. 15(3):330–50, Fall, 1946.

KEW, CLIFTON E., and CLINTON J. KEW. "Group Psychotherapy in a Church Setting," *Pastoral Psychology*. 1(10):31–37, January, 1951.

MACE, DAVID R. "The Childless Marriage," *McCall's*. 89(9):40, June, 1962.

MOORE, CARL A. "Biological Background of Male Sterility," *Fertility and Sterility*. 3(6):453–54, November–December, 1952.

POPENOE, P. "Eugenic Sterilization in California: Attitude of Patient's Relatives Toward the Operation," *Journal of Social Hygiene*. 14:271–80, May, 1928.

RUSSELL, MURRAY. "Can Male Infertility Be Prevented? Major Causes and Therapy," *Fertility and Sterility*. 5(30):256–62, May–June, 1954.

SCHWARTZ, BERNARD J. "Measurement of Castration Anxiety and Anxiety Over Loss of Love," *Journal of Personality*. 24:204–19, September–June, 1955–56.

SIMMONS, FRED A. "The Role of the Husband in Therapeutic Donor Insemination," *Fertility and Sterility*. 8(6):547–50, November–December, 1957.

STERN, A. "Ambivalence and Conception," *Fertility and Sterility*. 6(6):-540–42, November–December, 1955.

STURGISS, SOMERS H. "Higher Education, Uterine Fluid, and Sterility," *Fertility and Sterility*. 8(1):1–11, January–February, 1957.

TOMPKINS, PENDLETON. "Altitude and Fertility," *Fertility and Sterility*. 1(2):184–86, March–April, 1950.

TURNER, V. H., C. D. DAVIS and B. CARTER. "Correlation of Estimated Prognosis with Findings and Results in 750 Sterile Couples," *American Journal of Obstetrics and Gynecology*. 70:1189–98, December, 1955.

WEISMAN, ABNER I. "Fertilo-pak: A New Vaginal Tampon for Use in the Treatment of Lowered Fertility," *Fertility and Sterility*. 8(6):586–90, November–December, 1957.

WHITELAW, M. JAMES. "What Is Normal Female Fertility?" *Fertility and Sterility*. 6(2):103–11, March–April, 1955.

TESTS And MEASUREMENTS:
A SUPPLEMENTARY BIBLIOGRAPHY

Of the thousands of tests and measurements that have been made of fertility and sterility, most of them are medical and highly technical. The conclusions of medical research which are most relevant for the pastor in counseling the childless couple comprise a vital part of this writing. A summary of these tests and measurements is unnecessary and impracticable, if not impossible, and is not of specific significance in pastoral counseling.

The pastor who is especially interested in medical research on a specific aspect of sterility may obtain the desired information at a medical library of a local hospital or school of medicine. A sampling of the vast field of research on sterility is offered in the following references which may be used to supplement the annotated bibliography (Appendix A). The pastor may find these references helpful in his referral ministry.

FALLENLOVE, TOM M. "Roentgen Therapy in Anovulation and Sterility," *Fertility and Sterility*. 7(1):18–27, January–February, 1956.

JOEL, CHARLES A., and S. KORNHAUSER. "Influence of Antibiotics on the Motility of Spermatozoa," *Fertility and Sterility*. 7(5):430–39, September–October, 1956.

KISER, CLYDE V. *Group Differences in Urban Fertility: A Study Derived From the National Health Survey*. Baltimore: The Williams and Watkins Company, 1942. 284 pp.

LAMPE, E. H., and W. H. MASTERS. "Problems of Male Fertility: Effect of Frequent Ejaculation," *Fertility and Sterility*. 7(2):123–27, March–April, 1956.

MOORE, CARL R. "Biological Background of Male Sterility," *Fertility and Sterility*. 3(6):453–60, November–December, 1952.

POMERAT, C. M. "Assortive Marriage and Infertility," *Science*. 78:376, 1933.

TURNER, V. H., C. D. DAVID, J. ZANARTU and E. C. HAMBLESS. "Analysis of Clinical Data of 500 Childless Couples: Fertility Results," *Southern Medical Journal.* 44:628–38, July, 1951.

WARNER, M. P. "Pregnancy in Fifty-one Patients Diagnosed Incurably Sterile," *Journal of American Medical Women's Association.* 14:677–84, August, 1959.

WILSON, ROBERT B. "One Thousand Cases of Sterility," *Fertility and Sterility.* 4(4):292–99, July–August, 1953.

COMMUNITY, STATE
And NATIONAL RESOURCES

COMMUNITY

The pastor and the family physician are two primary resources of the childless couple. Both should be consulted, and from them the couple may derive many benefits, including referral to the indicated specialists, such as gynecologists, urologists, psychiatrists, social caseworkers, marriage counselors, hospitals, fertility clinics, agencies or societies. Childless couples may also secure first-hand information by telephoning or by visiting the local "Planned Parenthood" organization.

Adoption agencies usually know the location of the nearby and recommendable sterility clinics, and they may be relied upon to cooperate confidentially. Infertility services are available in hospitals and clinics in most of the larger cities throughout America. The Department of Public Welfare, the Council of Social Agencies, Marriage and Family Counseling centers, the Motherhood Advice Bureau and the Maternal Health Committee are also recommended local resources.

STATE

The local organizations, which are listed above, are usually coordinated from state headquarters which are frequently, and logically, located in the capital city of the state, and are usually listed in the telephone directory under the same title. The Department of Public Welfare and the Children's Home Society are two of the more prominent state resources.

State-supported universities, and particularly those institutions which have a school of medicine and a university press, may also prove to be a very valuable resource on the state level.

NATIONAL

The Planned Parenthood Federation of America, Incorporated, located at 501 Madison Avenue, New York 22, New York, is an excellent source of help. By writing to them a person may, for example, obtain considerable information through such pamphlets as *To Those Denied A Child* (10¢), *Infertility*, by Abraham Stone (10¢), and *How Can We Have A Baby?*, by Abraham Stone (5¢). By writing to them, a person may also secure the names and addresses of specific persons and organizations in a given community or state. Such information is accurate and "up-to-date," thanks to the 106 Affiliates of the Planned Parenthood Federation which are strategically located throughout the United States.

The American Society for the Study of Sterility, 920 South 19th Street, Birmingham 5, Alabama, specializes in the problems of the involuntarily childless couple. They are in an excellent position to give specific and specialized information. Their pamphlet, *Evaluation of the Barren Marriage: Minimal Procedure* (25¢), is highly recommended for an initial indoctrination to the problems of infertility, and is but one of the many aids which they offer.

The Public Affairs Committee, Incorporated, 22 East 38th Street, New York 16, New York, includes the problems of the childless couple in its manifold services, as effectively illustrated in their Pamphlet No. 137, *So You Want To Adopt A Baby*, by Ruth Carson (25¢).

The American Medical Association, 535 North Dearborn Street, Chicago 10, Illinois, publishes monthly in *Today's Health* a wealth of information, as verified by the following articles: "Hope for the Childless," by Clarissa Lorenz (October, 1951), "Helping the Childless," by Grace Naismith (February, 1954), "More Help For the Childless Couple," by Joseph D. Wassersug (September, 1947), "Why Fear Sterilization?" by Clarence J. Gamble (January, 1948), and "Emotional Block," by Alton L. Blakeslee.

Other significant national resources include the Children's Division of the Department of Public Welfare, American Association of Marriage Counselors, Maternity Health League and medical societies.

Perhaps the two best resources for keeping "up-to-date" on the latest developments are (1) *Fertility and Sterility*, a medical journal which is published every two months and which is available in the medical libraries of schools and hospitals, and (2) *The Cumulative Book Index*, which may be found in all of the better public and college libraries.

LIST Of
BIBLICAL REFERENCES

OLD TESTAMENT

Genesis 1:27–31; 2:24–25; 9:1;
16; 17; 18; 21; 25:21; 29;
30; 38.
Exodus 3:8.
Deuteronomy 4:29; 7:12–16;
23:1; 24:5; 25:5; 33:27.
Joshua 1:9.
Judges 5:30.
1 Samuel 1; 2; 3:13.
Job 1:21.

Psalms 16:8; 23; 25; 27; 31;
37:4–7; 40; 42; 46; 51; 63;
69:1–8; 71; 103; 113:9; 118;
123; 127; 130; 139.
Proverbs 7; 28:13; 30:16.
Ecclesiastes 3:1.
Isaiah 40:28–31; 41:13; 56:3–
5, 31–35.
Jeremiah 38:7–13.

NEW TESTAMENT

Matthew 4:4; 5:3–11, 17, 19,
28–30; 6:14–15, 27–34; 7:
11; 10:37–39; 11:28; 14;
19:5–6, 12; 22:24–28; 23:
24; 24:13; 25:5; 26:42.
Mark 2:17; 7:21.
Luke 1; 2:52; 8:15; 18:1; 22:
42.
John 5:14; 8:11, 32; 10:10;
12:47; 16:33.
Romans 3:23; 4:17; 5:1–8;

8:24–39; 12:1–2, 9, 12, 21;
14:1, 7–8, 23; 15:4–5.
1 Corinthians 3:6; 6:13–20;
7:5; 9:24–25; 12:26; 13:12.
2 Corinthians 4:13–18; 7:10.
Galatians 6:8–9.
Philippians 3:13–14; 4.
Hebrews 11:11.
James 1:2–4; 5:16.
2 Peter 1:5–8.
1 John 1:8–10; 4:18.

CHECK LIST
Of DO's And DON'T's

Do's only are as dangerous as roads without caution signs, and don't's only may so inhibit that progress is slowed by frustration or stopped completely by paralyzing fear. To know and to "hate . . . evil" is not enough. The counselor must also know the "good" in order to "hold fast" to it (Romans 12:9). By knowing both what not to do and what to do, the counselor is better prepared to "overcome evil with good" (Romans 12:21). Accordingly, for every don't there should be a comparable do, and, as they are thus associated in the concepts of the counselor, his efforts are channeled rather than blocked. The following do's and don't's are, therefore, listed together in the order in which they would normally be applicable from a developmental approach.

PRIOR TO MEDICAL DIAGNOSIS

(1) DON'T presuppose that childlessness necessarily infers a sterility problem, because some childless couples do not desire children. DO learn the parental desires of all the couples associated with the church if they are childless after two or more years of marriage.

(2) DON'T presuppose that the childless couple has a basic knowledge of the physiology of fertility and sterility. DO proceed as though the couple knew absolutely nothing about sterility.

(3) DON'T evaluate inner desires by external appearances which may deceitfully suggest wholesome adjustments. DO explore inner motivations during the initial phase of counseling.

(4) DON'T wait for the childless couple to seek pastoral guidance. DO take the initiative by going to them and paving the way for pastoral counseling when their infertility problem is in its incipient

stage, and when they are young enough for a more favorable prognosis.

(5) *DON'T* presume that couples who state that they do not desire children have a happy vocational adjustment. *DO* explore with these couples the thinking and motivation supporting their decision in order to help them to a positive vocational adjustment, or to uncover their true feelings that lie behind the protective walls of the false "front" which states, "we don't want children."

(6) *DON'T* endanger a weak counselor-counselee relationship with questions which probe into sensitive areas of sexual intimacy. *DO* enhance rapport and know the counselee well before exploring previous taboos so that questioning will be timely and well received.

(7) *DON'T* assume the role of an omniscient, omnipotent judge. *DO* explicitly state and clearly demonstrate a permissive, accepting, human, understanding role as a representative of God.

(8) *DON'T* hesitate to use the Scriptures because this is a part of the pastor's accepted role. *DO* seek an alignment of their thinking to Scriptural teachings because both God and the couple expect this of the pastor.

(9) *DON'T* assume the medical role of diagnostician and therapist. *DO* function clearly within the religious role in the spirit of Christ.

(10) *DON'T* dodge religious issues in an effort to be "nondirective." *DO* confront the theological, ethical and moral concepts which burden the couple because among other reasons, by so doing, the pastor achieves his best initial means to facilitating communication.

(11) *DON'T* limit counseling to a "one at a time" approach. *DO,* whenever possible, interview the couple together at the onset and at the conclusion of formal counseling, and utilize the available means for group guidance.

(12) *DON'T* attribute to the will of God purposes which are alien to his character. *DO* show the love, grace, justice and impartial consistency of God in explaining the Creator's physical laws of fertility.

(13) *DON'T* give "silent consent" to statements or to inferences that to seek medical aid to fertility is to oppose the God of "nature." *DO* support referrals to physicians for diagnostic testing with the reassurance that such corrective action is an act of reverent trust in

the Creator, an effort to cooperate with his divine providence as manifest in the physiology of fertility.

(14) *DON'T* presuppose that the childless couple should have children. *DO* help them to find their vocational destiny within the will of God, because this is their means to maximum fulfillment.

(15) *DON'T* by-pass the purposes of God in marriage. *DO* correct misconceptions such as those concerning the "one flesh," unitive purposes of marriage and the "be fruitful and multiply," procreative possibilities of marriage.

(16) *DON'T* assume the role of a physician by going into the medical details of the physiology of reproduction. *DO,* when sufficiently informed, negate medical misconceptions which stifle initiative, and indoctrinate them in the basic essentials of fertility.

(17) *DON'T* try to meet the total needs of the couple alone. *DO* refer them to the appropriate medical authority and support the referral with the assurance that it is better to know for sure than to remain in doubt.

(18) *DON'T* concur with the counselee's fatalistic disregard of conditioning factors in his self-diagnosis. *DO* explore the emotional roots of the couple's diagnostic presuppositions.

(19) *DON'T* attempt to reassure with generalities or with trite platitudes. *DO* reassure specifically and realistically, both in content and in implication.

(20) *DON'T* refer the wife only for medical diagnosis. *DO* enlist the cooperation and participation of the husband as well in the diagnostic testing.

(21) *DON'T* terminate the counseling relationship with the medical referral. *DO* maintain unbroken relationships and "stay with" the couple through every phase of their sterility problem.

(22) *DON'T* refer prematurely. *DO* refer the couple to their family physician first.

DURING MEDICAL DIAGNOSIS

(1) *DON'T* wait for the couple to contact their pastor. *DO* take the initiative rather than to let them become acutely tense.

(2) *DON'T* discredit the couple's opposition to certain means of diagnostic testing, such as the post-coital test. *DO* inform them of

alternate tests and, thereby, encourage them to complete their diagnostic survey.

(3) *DON'T* regard lightly the prolonged diagnostic testing period of waiting. *DO* strengthen their patience by using the Scriptures on a prescription basis.

UPON DISCOVERING THE CAUSES OF STERILITY

(1) *DON'T* wait for the couple to contact the pastor. *DO* seek an interview with them as soon as practicable after they learn the results of their fertility examination.

(2) *DON'T* attempt to resolve psychogenic sterility alone. *DO* seek to enlist the services of a psychiatrist for such couples.

(3) *DON'T* underestimate the emotional impact of learning the causes of permanent sterility. *DO* regard their crisis as complex bereavement and counsel accordingly in a controlled relationship for several weeks.

(4) *DON'T* state or imply that human efforts are negated by the presence of an unknown or "X"-factor in sterility. *DO* reassure with facts on the rapid progress in contemporary research on sterility.

(5) *DON'T* neglect the powerful resources of the Scriptures and of prayer. *DO* note the similarities and differences between Scriptural and contemporary attitudes toward sterility, and, by the use of the Bible and prayer in counseling, lead the couple to identify with sterile persons of the Scriptures whose attitudes are positive.

(6) *DON'T* "non-directively" evade the responsibilities of pastoral guidance in such moral issues as masturbation for fertility testing, infidelity, separation, divorce or artificial insemination. *DO* enlighten without coercively imposing the convictions of the counselor upon the counselee.

(7) *DON'T* offer unrealistic hope in considering the alternative of adoption. *DO* examine the requirements for adoption, the proportion of applicants to the number of babies available for adoption, the legal aspects of adoption and the need for patient perseverance.

(8) *DON'T* encourage childless couples to begin adoptive procedures before the resolution of their sterility trauma. *DO* explore their narcissistic and other negative motives for desiring children, as well as the possibilities of having children of their own after successful fertility testing and treatment.

(9) *DON'T* terminate the counseling relationship with the referral to an adoption agency. *DO* maintain a permanent relationship which "stands by" them in the prolonged months of stress and strain.

(10) *DON'T* regard pastoral counseling of individuals as adequate for their emotion of loneliness. *DO* seek to bring groups of childless couples into either new or established groups which are skillfully guided to meet their mutual needs.

(11) *DON'T* limit the consideration of alternatives to those which the counselor deems most advantageous to the sterile couple. *DO* explore with the barren couple *all* the alternatives to childlessness, which include artificial insemination, adoption, temporary parenthood of the foster parents, of daily baby-sitting with the same child or children, of teaching children and of working with children in the church or community.

(12) *DON'T* leave the prayers of the childless couple to chance. *DO* teach them to pray realistically, intelligently, maturely and effectively, and to walk with God in keeping with answered prayer.

(13) *DON'T* minimize the importance of the couple's sense of sin and guilt, and their felt needs for a "new start." *DO* render a most valuable ministry toward meeting their felt needs by recognizing the universality of sin, and by leading such couples to confess, to repent, to be reconciled to God and to conform to His Way. In so doing, *DON'T* condemn; *DO* express concern for their maximum fulfillment.

(14) *DON'T* leave the vocational choice of parenthood to superficial thinking. *DO* consider parenthood in both the initial and the closing phases of counseling in the light of eugenic, personal, psychological, time, economic and environmental factors under the prayerful guidance of the Holy Spirit.

INDEX